SACRAMENTO MOTORCYCLING

A CAPITAL CITY TRADITION

KIMBERLY REED EDWARDS

Foreword by Rich Ostrander, Fort Sutter Motorcycle Club
Introduction by Ken Magri and the Capital City Motorcycle Club

Published by The History Press
Charleston, SC
www.historypress.com

Copyright © 2021 by Kimberly Reed Edwards
All rights reserved

First published 2021

Manufactured in the United States

ISBN 9781467143035

Library of Congress Control Number: 2021937211

Notice: The information in this book is true and complete to the best of our knowledge. It is offered without guarantee on the part of the author or The History Press. The author and The History Press disclaim all liability in connection with the use of this book.

All rights reserved. No part of this book may be reproduced or transmitted in any form whatsoever without prior written permission from the publisher except in the case of brief quotations embodied in critical articles and reviews.

CONTENTS

Foreword, by Richard L. Ostrander, Fort Sutter Motorcycle Club	5
The Durable Code of Early Sacramento Motorcyclists	7
Preface	9
Acknowledgements	11
Introduction, by Ken Magri and the Capital City Motorcycle Club	15
The Remarkable Early Years	17
How Sacramento Became a Leader in the Prewar Motorcycle Years	42
Law Enforcement: The *Rat-ta-ta-tat* that Ruled the Road and Haunted Speeders	64
After World War I: The Making of a Motorcycle Mecca	79
Sacramento's Love Affair with Spectator Sports	98
Chrome and Polish: The Groundbreaking Sacramento Cyclettes	121
Before and After World War II: Heroes of Mud, Skies and Track	134
Symbols of the Mid-Century Sacramento Motorcycle Scene	157
Selected Bibliography	183
Index	187
About the Author	191

When not riding or working on motorcycles, Whitie Tompkins sketched the objects he loved the most, such as the machines themselves, leaving a vibrant legacy of the first fifty years of the sport here in Sacramento. 1947. *Gaylene Tompkins.*

FOREWORD

Before radio became one of the main sources of entertainment, and television was still over the horizon, sporting events captured large numbers of spectators. One of the largest was motorcycle racing on board tracks and dirt ovals, hill climbs and club field events.

Northern California's Bay Area and the San Joaquin Valley had racetracks in almost every city and town. Most of the events were sponsored by local dealers and or clubs. Riders from near and far, plus Joe and Joanne Citizen who would never sit in a saddle, would attend these activities, usually held on a Saturday or Sunday afternoon.

Through Kimberly Reed Edwards's book, you will be taken back to the golden age of motorcycling in Northern California, especially the Sacramento area, from the turn of the century to 1960. You will meet local motorcycle dealers, repair shop operators, well-known racers, everyday riders and local clubs. You will experience their lifestyle and adventures.

So find a comfortable chair, sit back and enjoy the ride through one of the most interesting and exciting times in motorcycling history.

—Richard L. Ostrander,
Historian Emeritus, Fort Sutter Motorcycle Club (founded in 1934),
Chapter of the Antique Motorcycle Club of America,
"To preserve, restore, exhibit motorcycles that are more than 35 years old"

THE DURABLE CODE OF EARLY SACRAMENTO MOTORCYCLISTS

Courage
Hardy Tompkins, living on Front Street with his one-hundred-year-old grandmother from Sonora, Mexico, scored the day's highest one-mile time over riders of national fame on a Jefferson in 1913 at the California State Fairgrounds. Ads called him the man "who traveled 80 mph." Two years later, he died of tuberculosis at age twenty-four, just months after competing in another race.

Fellowship
William A. Langley, charter member of the Sacramento Motorcycle Club, advocated motorcycling as a means to bring people together. One of Sacramento's earliest motorcycle dealers, he led coed excursions around Northern California. In his pocket, he carried a list of traffic ordinances. National racing stars such as Charles "Fearless" Balke came to Sacramento because of Langley's reputation for putting on good races.

Goodwill
Frank A. Woodson, son of an original Capital City Wheelman who was also a respected journalist for the *Sacramento Union*, served as the town's first humane officer. As leader of the Sacramento motorcycle brigade, he set up road signs for endurance races so riders could stay on course. Named as state referee by the Federation of American Motorcyclists, he traveled to the Bay Area to recruit riders for local races.

The Durable Code of Early Sacramento Motorcyclists

Independence
Mittie Landreth arrived in Sacramento alone at age eighteen after journeying from her home in Arkansas to Texas in a covered wagon. In 1893, she opened a bicycle shop at 913 K Street. Although she never added motorcycles to her inventory, she operated alongside male two-wheeled dealers on J and K Streets, modeling the spirit required in an unfolding mechanized world.

Sacrifice
Break-out star Reed Orr, age nineteen and only child of an Oak Park general practitioner, died in 1912 at the San Jose Speedway after zooming to stardom in races in Sacramento. Orr's fellow members of the National Guard accompanied his casket to East Lawn Cemetery on Folsom Boulevard, deploying the firing guard at a graveside service in Orr's honor.

Service
Emil O. Putzman of Putzman & Hoffman Sporting Goods sold bicycles and motorcycles after moving here from San Francisco and Oakland, where he ran enameling businesses. A former U.S. marine in the Spanish-American War, he coordinated patriotic celebrations at the request of Sacramento mayor Albert Elkus. He oversaw youth competitions, including baseball and track and field.

Teamwork
Irene Kaminsky financed clubhouses for two local motorcycle clubs with her husband, Julius. Stressing the value of getting along and working as a unit, she guided the Sacramento Cyclettes, a women's motorcycle group organized in 1938. She gave inspiring speeches and shared her poetry. In mid-life, she learned to golf. She started the junior golf program and was the first woman elected to the Sacramento Golf Council.

Vision
Lauren Stuart Upson, vice-president of Kimball-Upson Sporting Goods and founder of Del Paso Country Club, navigated the relationship between merchants, civic leadership, riders and the police department. An early Capital City Wheelman and active in the chamber of commerce, he led the development of many landmarks (e.g., the Memorial Auditorium). Sacramento's first radio show was broadcasted from his store.

PREFACE

Sacramento sits on a rich history of cycling intertwined with merchants, politicians and civic leaders. Names lie buried just outside of Sacramento's commonly known past, found best by piecing together newspapers, photos, government records and surviving artifacts. These lost names all played important roles in the development of an exciting new industry. They asked for nothing but to do what they loved to do: ride, race, repair, sell or talk about motorcycles.

The people who appreciate motorcycles belong to a special group. They worship the roar, the scent, the vibration, the shiny chrome and the feeling of freedom afforded by flying through open air. The world looks different from the seat of a bike. The rider feels as close to nature as one can get on a machine. I am privileged to capture and memorialize the legends of Sacramento as a part of our city's history.

I dedicate this book to all the Northern California men and women who rode, promoted, sold, rebuilt—and died doing what they loved to do—all who traversed the trails, chased the clock or trailed one another through dirt, ditches and streams. Without fear of broken bones or mud-splattered clothes, they steadied their handlebars to dominate the tracks, the roads and the slopes surrounding our city.

Special thanks to lead technical advisor Rich Ostrander, historian emeritus of the Fort Sutter Chapter of the Antique Motorcycle Club of America, who answered my many questions with knowledge and patience. Ken Magri, son of racer and Harley-Davidson dealer Armando Magri,

Preface

The author getting ready for a ride on an Indian Chief at 1520 16th Street, 1952. *Jim Reed Archives.*

supplied photos, history and valuable opinions at every turn. Ralph Venturino, historian of the Capital City Motorcycle Club, generously shared club records and primary sources. He met with me many times, enabling me to examine documents and paraphernalia representing the riding spirit. Able writer and RustMag.com publisher Michael Blanchard, racer Rich Hardmeyer and longtime enthusiasts Steve Tompkins, Jerry Bland, Gaylene Tompkins and others made sure that I got the information I needed.

And special thanks to my dad for my own early memories of the sound of his foot striking the kick starter on his Indian Chief. This repetitive motion, followed by a fierce growl and the scent of burning oil and gas, meant that all was well in the world to a little girl on her father's lap. I compiled this account for him and all the others up in that "Great Motorcycle Sky."

Saluting the heroes of early Sacramento motorcycling history.

ACKNOWLEDGEMENTS

LEAD PHOTO TECHNICAL ADVISOR: Rich Ostrander, historian emeritus, Fort Sutter Motorcycle Club

PHOTO ADVISORS: Ken Magri, Michael Blanchard, Rich Hardmeyer, Jimmie Jones, Jerry Bland, Anthony Martinis, Steve Tompkins and Gaylene Tompkins

PARTIAL LIST OF CONTRIBUTORS:
Chris and Cary Agajanian, Ascot Motorsports Products, LLC
Ross Alzina, grandson of Hap Alzina
Marnie Anderson, great-granddaughter of Archie Rife
Bud Bagdasarian, son of Harold Bagdasarian
Bambi Barker, relative of E.O. Putzman
Vince Bertolucci, Bertolucci's Body and Fender Shop
Michael Blanchard, writer and publisher, RustMag.com
Keith Brooks, President, Capital City Motorcycle Club
Kim Brown, daughter of Walt Vaughan
Paul Brown, Sacramento Police Officers Association
William Burg, historian, author of seven books, including *Wicked Sacramento*
Kevin Cadwell, son of "Red" Cadwell
Tim Comstock, Del Paso Country Club
Tim Cottrell, Del Paso Country Club Anniversary Book
Terry Cox, College Cyclery

Acknowledgements

Alan Dow, Fort Sutter Motorcycle Club
Don Emde, racer, historian, author and publisher
Vhonn Ryan Encarnacion, PhotoSource
Donald Gilbertson, Sacramento Police Department (Ret.)
Kelli Gonsoulin, rider
Tom Green, Fort Sutter Motorcycle Club
Rich Hardmeyer, former president, Fort Sutter Motorcycle Club
Kim Hayden, Center for Sacramento History
Jan Selby Holden, daughter of Carl Selby
Jane Jackson, wife of Ron Adams
Alan and Craig Johnson, motorcycle enthusiasts
Jimmie Jones, Fort Sutter Motorcycle Club
Mark Loewen, President, Fort Sutter Motorcycle Club
Ken Magri, writer, curator of "Armando Magri" Facebook page, son of Armando Magri
John Markley, Fort Sutter Motorcycle Club; Board Member, Antique Motorcycle Club of America
Vince Martinico, collector, motorcycle historian
Anthony Martinis, rider and former motorcycle shop employee
Rick Mattos, CHP Museum and author, *California Highway Patrol* (Images of America)
Motorcycle Hall of Fame (AMA) Museum staff
Tom Motter, author and publisher, *Sacramento: Dirt Capital of the West*
Shawn Murray, Capital City Motorcycle Club
Rich Ostrander, author and historian emeritus, Fort Sutter Motorcycle Club
Katie Pond, District 36/Polka Dots Motorcycle Club
Chris Price, historian, Antique Motorcycle Club of America and blogger, archivemoto.com
Ed Quint, motorcycle enthusiast
Norris Rancourt, racer and founder of Carmichael Honda and Rancourt Motor Sports
Art Reed, George W. Reed Archives
Dan and Doug Reed, sons of Jim Reed
Sacramento Railroad Museum research staff
James Sadilek, Fort Sutter Motorcycle Club
Ed Schenken, Fort Sutter Motorcycle Club
James Scott, archivist, Sacramento Public Library, and co-author, *World War I and the Sacramento Valley*

Acknowledgements

Margie Siegel, author, *Harley-Davidson: A History of the World's Most Famous Motorcycle*
Deborah Smith, daughter of Cy Homer
Shasta Smith, the Vintage Monkey, Motorcycle Specialists
James Springer, motorcycle and car author
Tracy Stahlman, historian, Fort Sutter Motorcycle Club
Cheryl Stapp, author of six historical books, including *Sacramento Chronicles: A Golden Past*
John L. Stein, journalist: *Cycle World, Motorcyclist, Autoweek, Vintage Motorsport, Motorcycle Classics, Sports Car Market*
Ray Stith, District 36, Road Rider Division California State delegate, American Motorcycle Association
Kathy Stricklin, "Vintage Arden Arcade" Facebook Group
Carol Sutherland, daughter of Orrin Hall
Hal Tacker, writer and artist
Joan Kibbey Taylor, historian, Del Paso Country Club
Gaylene Tompkins, daughter-in-law of Whitie Tompkins
Steve Tompkins, son of Shorty Tompkins
Bob Turek, Fort Sutter Motorcycle Club
Ralph Venturino, historian, Capital City Motorcycle Club
William Villano, Center for Sacramento History
Sally Zentner, great-niece of E.M. Brown

INTRODUCTION

In 1960, when I was seven years old and barely aware enough of the world to sense the good old days of motorcycling in Northern California, I experienced firsthand what motorcycling was like in Sacramento. Being the child of Sacramento Harley-Davidson dealer Armando Magri meant that motorcycle field meets and poker runs were just a normal part of my upbringing.

Field meets unfolded as all-day picnics, organized by enthusiastic local motorcycle clubs. The day was filled with friendly competitive games on bikes. The "run and ride" was a foot race to a motorcycle, which had to be started and ridden back to the starting line. The "Australian pursuit" put riders in a big circular track, trying to pass one another to eliminate them. The "balloon chase" had passengers swatting at balloons on the backs of other passengers.

But my favorite motorcycle game to watch was the slow race, which was exactly what it sounded like. Riders went so slowly that they would eventually fall over sideways. It was hilarious to watch. "It was just good clean fun," said Merrill Wolhart, whom I visited recently. At ninety-seven, Wolhart is the oldest living member of the Capital City Motorcycle Club.

Poker runs were like a scavenger hunt, at several stops on route to a field meet, for bags filled with stapled playing cards. The fifth card came at the final destination for the meet. After unfolding everyone's cards, the best poker hand won a small trophy. "They would give out a trophy for just

Introduction

about anything," said Wolhart, his smile grown even wiser over the years. If anyone would know, he would.

Collared riding shirts and turned-up blue jeans were the fashion back when I was growing up. I wore a black satin riding cap with a little white brim. Sitting on the gas tank of a Harley-Davidson panhead, with my father jockeying the bike behind me, I followed his directions. He would point to a number on the hand-shifter and let me change gears for him.

In hindsight, those days represent the end of an era—the glorious days of Sacramento motorcycling. In subsequent decades, chopped motorcycles, outlaw bikers and patched leathers would usher in an edgier phase of motorcycling, bringing with it a loss of innocence among the general public about who exactly motorcyclists were.

This book takes a nostalgic look back, starting more than a century ago, to the decades when motorcycles inspired adventurous locals. It follows their exploits through the first part of the twentieth century and showcases the development of Sacramento's motorcycle culture, from the gas-scented garage of the shop mechanic to the evolving fashions of women who preceded the national Motor Maid organization. It was a time that is slowly drifting away from our collective thoughts and memories, as we sojourn further into the 2000s.

On behalf of my father, who loved motorcycles as much as life, and on behalf of the Capital City Motorcycle Club of which he was an honorary member, as well as all motorcycle enthusiasts, I welcome this book.

—Ken Magri,
son of racer/dealer Armando Magri (Honorary Lifetime Member),
Capital City Motorcycle Club (founded in 1913 upon merger of
Capital City Wheelmen with Sacramento Motorcycle Club),
District 36, American Motorcyclist Association

THE REMARKABLE EARLY YEARS

I n October 1911, as the sun moved over the plaza at 10th and J Streets, eighty motorcycles lined up for the parade to kick off the Greater Sacramento Annexation Jubilee motorcycle meet. Horns honked and cowbells jangled. The breeze carried a mix of burning oil and coal as motors spit, brakes hissed and metal clanked from nearby railyards. The band struck up a repertoire of songs: "California Girl March" and "In the Good Old Days Gone By." As the motorcycles rumbled down J toward 15th Street, they struck up a symphony in harmony with the band. Spectators leaned in to get a better look. Fenders glinted in and out of the sun, lowering behind the men crouched atop the roofs. Handlebars shook from furrows in the street. William A. Langley angled his Kodak camera to get good shots to post outside his Excelsior Motorcycle shop. Stu Upson of Kimball-Upson Sporting Goods brandished the latest catalogue displaying his Pope motorcycle. Hiram Cameron Jr., strolling up from 4th and J, waved a commemorative glass plate depicting the Indian motorcycle, on display in his showroom.

MotoTown Sacramento

As the crowd gathered in these days before radio and television, the "motorized" bikes proved yet again to fascinate Sacramentans. These machines were, after all, a novel new mode of travel and diversion. Faster than a bicycle and

Families and friends spent afternoons visiting and enjoying the new freedom afforded by motorcycles. *Vince Martinico.*

cheaper than an automobile, they demanded less upkeep than a horse and buggy. Families enjoyed Sunday rides in the country to see friends and relatives.

From the time motorcycles first appeared here, spectators packed the stands to get a glimpse of the "fire-belching beasts." Residents turned out at Recreation Park and the Oak Park Velodrome. The 1901 grand opening of the Velodrome—one-eighth of a mile at a twenty-eight-degree slant—featured spinning wheels ridden by gravity-defying champs from New York and Colorado as fine music played. Soon the Capital City Wheelmen began appending motorcycle races to its slates of bicycle competitions held at Agricultural Park at G and 22nd Streets. Even the automobile dealers club occasionally slipped motorcycles into their racing palette.

Indeed, competitive racing wasn't new to Sacramento. In fact, the town basked in a growing image of a glorious racing town. Two decades of success in hosting and participating in bicycle races, and now motorcycle races, provided a built-in network of companion riding towns: Stockton, Fresno, Bakersfield, Tracy, Oakland, San Francisco, San Jose, Marysville, Woodland, Galt, Auburn and Chico, to name a few. Dedicated motorcycle races at the State Fair's new Agricultural Park on Stockton Boulevard

A Capital City Tradition

guaranteed a thrill every time. Trolleys from downtown to Oak Park ran back and forth, bursting with racegoers. Some rode their own motorcycles, filling the adjacent "motorcycle lot" with every brand that had ever passed through Sacramento: Thor, Excelsior, Racycle, Pope, Yale, Duck, Thor, Indian, Curtiss, Merkel or Dayton. The Cyclone was soon to come.

If anyone thought that Sacramento's reputation was a West Coast secret, they didn't know star sprinter Charles Balke from Illinois. When he came to California in 1911 to race at Oakland's new motordrome, he couldn't resist coming here to see Excelsior dealer William A. Langley, known to put on good races. No track compared to Sacramento's—not just in Balke's eyes, but in those of other rising greats: Robert Perry, Don Johns, Armstrong, Collins, Wolters, McGinley, Broderick, De Rosier and Ray Seymour. Even Albert "Shrimp" Burns, the Oakdale kid who would become a member of the Harley-Davidson "Wrecking Crew," would skid on Sacramento's oval in 1913 in his first race at age fifteen. Both Burns and Balke, relishing their soaring national fame, would earn their place in the annals of motorcycle history before losing their lives on other tracks, as did many other racers.

Spectators walked through the "motorcycle lot" at Agricultural Park before the start of a race. *Capital City Motorcycle Club.*

William A. Langley's 10th Street shop attracted star racers such as Charles "Fearless" Balke, on an Excelsior 7, 1911. Behind Balke stands his wife, Edith, in a coat and Langley's wife, Ellen, in gloves. *Capital City Motorcycle Club.*

The local Excelsior team, who rode for Langley, included *(from left to right)* Ivan Carbine, Elvin Shoemaker, "Flying" Dick Galloway and Roy Emery. *From* Motorcycle and Bicycle Illustrated.

A Capital City Tradition

On the day after the Annexation Jubilee parade, two thousand spectators poured into the Agricultural Park grandstand ready for a show. Honorary starter "Strong Mayor" Marshall R. Beard shook hands with race judge, Stu Upson of Kimball-Upson Sporting Goods. The race had been billed as the best ever, with some of the world's greatest pros coming. As it turned out, the train bringing the national Excelsior team was late, so Ray Seymour of Los Angeles on an Indian battled out the five-mile race with fewer competitors, prevailing over Collins and Albright. Seymour also beat the track record at a fraction over fifty-one seconds.

Two days later, the crowd was back when Balke arrived, ready to clash with Seymour in the five mile. At the signal, they and other contestants including Collins guided their bikes to the line, with pushers in place at the rear of the wheels. The crowd held its breath as it watched the raised flag flutter in the slightest of wind. When the flag dropped, the bikes fired off so fast that the nearby fence quivered. Howls arose in the grandstand. The crowd rose to its feet, where it stayed, swaying with the gyrations on the track. The synchronized screeches of the bikes separated into shrills at the curves, blending again when the pack attacked the straightaways. On the fourth lap, Seymour bumped the machine of W.T. Collins and "smacked his hand on his gasoline tank" on the back stretch, although this move was likely missed by spectators. Collins, according to newspaper reports, "showed his gameness by continuing the race and entering the rest of the schedule with a hand that was numb from pain." Meanwhile, Balke's Excelsior clobbered Seymour, winning 3 out of 5 races in the set, but Seymour got his way by beating Collins for second place. Still, Balke bested the track record that Seymour had claimed. In the Amateur race, San Francisco's Hap Alzina and "Captain" Chester Scott of the Sacramento Motorcycle Club grabbed first and second, while Trapper of the Indian Agency would snap up the special club championship. Dealer Langley's Excelsior team tore up the oval to make the usual good showing in the special five-mile race for Sacramento Motorcycle Club members.

In spite of the two-day delay for some of the races, the *Sacramento Bee* of October 23, 1911, noted that the Sacramento Motorcycle Club was "much elated at the way the Sacramento people took to the motorcycle races and in the near future intend to have another Sunday of racing."

After the race, Monarch Diamond Oil capitalized on Balke's fame with a *Sacramento Bee* ad: "Charles Balke who holds the motorcycle speed record used Monarch Diamond Oil in Sacramento Motorcycle Races." Under the illustration appeared the names of dealer Langley and local garages promoting the racer, the oil and the wonderful new sport.

The Capital City Wheelmen and the Sacramento Motorcycle Club

Sacramento's glowing racing history originated in large part from the Capital City Wheelmen. Formed in 1886, this club was the second-oldest bicycle club in Northern California, if not the state. Members and associates illuminated anyone's social gathering: McClatchy, Hale, Breuner, Elkus, Harris Weinstock, Frank Ruhstaller, McDonald, Canfield and Elliott, to name a few.

Members rode "wheel ways," paved roads for which they lobbied. They prided themselves in the paths of crushed and oiled gravel extending from Brighton to Folsom, paid with funds levied on members at one dollar each. Teams triumphed at contests all over Northern California. Younger riders also swam, picnicked and enjoyed river rides together while serving as informal apprentices of a socially connected Wheelmen "old guard." This eldership handed down sacred club traditions: music, singing, whist matches and speeches by leading merchants and officials at the prestigious clubhouse, occupying an entire floor of the Sacramento Bank on J between 4th and 5th Streets.

In the spring of 1911, a new club appeared on the competition scene: the Sacramento Motorcycle Club, open to everyone who shared the interest. This club wished to promote motorcycle riding, aid in the good roads movement and cooperate with organizations to preserve courtesies of the road. The Armory Building at 6th and L hosted weekly meetings. Appealing to a younger group of riders, applications for membership came by way of "Langley's Motorcycle Store." Anyone of good moral standing could join. The dues of three "lady members" were waived. Membership totaled forty-nine, including Chester Scott, Hardy Tompkins and Reed Orr. According to an official of the Western Federation of Motorcycles, the sport was an equalizer—where "the poorest man can become an expert." Outings took members to Folsom on "a beautiful boulevard" or the fruit country of Auburn and Placerville. A run to a Stockton race brought out twenty-two members and fifteen women.

But when the Sacramento Motorcycle Club began publicizing its own competitions, the Wheelmen took special note. After all, theirs was the club accustomed to dominating race headlines. Sensing their own vulnerability in the face of a growing motorcycle trend, the savvy Wheelmen knew that they needed a plan. Of late, their club lacked vitality. There were murmurs of complacency and aging membership rolls and

A Capital City Tradition

Young men and women in the Sacramento Motorcycle Club made day runs to all corners of the Sacramento area, circa 1912. *Capital City Motorcycle Club.*

Breuner's at 6th and K Street served as backdrop for three half-clowning unidentified Sacramento Motorcycle Club members, showing off their Excelsior and Yale motorcycles. *Vince Martinico.*

activities that had grown more social than sporty. At their twenty-fifth-anniversary celebration, Wheelman Joseph A. Woodson kicked off the usual "high jinx and stag" with a boisterous roast. As laughter broke into song, Woodson, one of the most prominent journalists on the Pacific Coast and an esteemed writer for the *Sacramento Union* and the *Record* before that, urged fellow Wheelmen to consider opening their charter to motorcyclists. When Woodson spoke, members listened. Perhaps they could start a motorcycle "arm" of the Wheelmen. This route to a fresh slate of members would come best through the Sacramento Motorcycle Club. Such a proposition had merit, as the new club lacked the political muscle required to prosper, while the Wheelmen had the connections. The clubs each offered something the other needed. But the idea would require consultation with the other club. So when leaders of both organizations met, they agreed to try an informal "courtship."

Birth of the Capital City Motorcycle Club

The first teamed event of the two clubs came on April 21, 1912. The "Come on and See Motorcycle Races" featured single- and twin-cylinder motorcycles, five- and ten-mile races and a special Stockton-Sacramento "first on the coast" twenty-five-mile relay for the coveted Weinstock Lubin Cup. Track tenders pampered the soil to ensure "spectator safety when the cycles hit a high rate of speed." Newspapers such as the *Star*, the *Sacramento Union* and the *Sacramento Bee* churned out projections of a race no one dared miss: "Entries coming from all clubs on the coast," "reckless daredevils" and "marvels on motorcycles" with "utter disregard for danger."

On the day of the race, 1,500 people filed into the Agricultural Park grandstand. A band played "The Belle of Venice," kicking off a continuous stream of entertainment. Wheelman Joseph A. Woodson officiated, along with Superior Court judge C.N. Post, an important Wheelman ally. Local boys Chester Scott, Dick Galloway and Reed Orr of the Sacramento Motorcycle Club fired up their nerves to decimate the Stockton team on the track.

In a rousing startup of dust and smoke, Scott, Galloway and Orr took off. Cheers shook the stands in support for the hometown team. The Sacramento boys prevailed. As the sun shifted over spectators' heads, nineteen-year-old Orr returned to the oval to score more wins in the twin-cylinder five- and ten-mile races. A three-mile novelty race, designed to captivate the public,

A Capital City Tradition

Left: The Capital City Wheelmen and the Sacramento Motorcycle Club teamed up to sponsor a race at Agricultural Park. *Center for Sacramento History.*

Below: Reed Orr, thought to be one of these competitors, devoured a piece of pie in between laps in a 1912 novelty race. *Center for Sacramento History.*

required competitors to halt after each mile to consume a treat before jumping into the next mile. Orr won that race too, meriting four wins and overnight stardom.

Six weeks later, when Orr competed at the San Jose Speedway, a fallen pipe caused him and San Jose's W.F. Baker to topple off their frames. Riders behind collapsed on top of them. Orr and Baker died instantly. Hearing of his only child's accident, Dr. Alexander Orr, an Oak Park general practitioner from Kentucky, rushed to the site of the accident. The boy's mother, Loretta, was described as overcome with grief. Since Orr was a member of the National Guard of California, the Company G "firing squad" accompanied his casket to East Lawn Cemetery. There they laid his remains in the shade of a cedar, just yards from a favorite Wheelmen run along Folsom Boulevard.

In spite of the loss of a young champion, Sacramentans' thirst for motorcycling soared. No amount of sad news seemed to quell the pursuit of a promising new sport.

Back at the Wheelman clubhouse, over plates of oysters, olives, cold turkey and fancy cakes, President Fred Pearl squeezed between Judge Post and Mayor Beard to grab the gavel to open the meeting. Leaders of the Sacramento Motorcycle Club sat among them. When the plates were cleared, cigars passed hands. The Wheelmen baseball team raised their gloves in support of the visiting club. A merger of the two clubs seemed more likely by the day. Wheelman and Civil War veteran Harrison Bennett voiced belief in "the boys" and swelling membership rolls, with a promise to return the coming year, when he turned age seventy-two.

Having co-sponsored a successful racing event, the two clubs formed a committee to track legislation benefiting riders, dealers and manufacturers. The clubs desired to influence motorcycle policies. Standing in front of flags of the Sacramento Motorcycle Club and the Western Federation of Motorcyclists, four representatives vowed to serve: Adrian ten Bosch, president of the Sacramento Motorcycle Club; Clarence Pixley, chief clerk of the California Board of Education; C.C. White, a businessman; and Hiram "Holy" Cameron, Indian dealer.

In the following months, the two clubs launched a series of public events. A motorcycle "carnival" of five dozen decorated machines stoked the throng assembled along J and K Streets. A "ribbon run" brought teams from surrounding towns sporting distinct colors, with yellow designated for Sacramento. The Wheelmen clubhouse at the Sacramento Bank drew three hundred people to dance amid ferns and potted plants laced with club colors of gold, garnet and black. A prestigious printed

A Capital City Tradition

The Wheelmen and the Sacramento Motorcycle Club joined forces to track legislation affecting riders and roads: Adrian ten Bosch (*left*), Indian dealer "Holy" Cameron (*back*), Clarence Pixley (*front*) and C.C. White (*right*). *Center for Sacramento History.*

program listed waltzes ("Take Me Back to the Garden of Love"), two-steps ("You Can't Expect Kisses from Me") and Schottisches ("Cuddle Up a Little Closer").

Endurance runs, track races and hill climbs kept members engaged and with their cycles at the ready. Chester Scott, one of the best riders in town, placed first on his Jefferson at a hill climb at Rattlesnake Bridge and Auburn Road. His time, 5:48, was a minute faster than his nearest rival on a Thor. The next highest set of scores belonged to the Indian riders, among them fourteen-year-old Emil Fabian, who lived at 1520 M Street.

All events drew newspaper coverage by Wheelmen members who worked in journalism and newspaper advertising. Updates on planned races either shot or dripped out of the newsroom with just the right hype to hook potential attendees: "Entry list swollen higher than any other meet in state" and the usual "First time on coast…at speeds seldom witnessed." Expected out-of-towners bolstered turnout predictions, motivating fans who wouldn't dare miss a race. "San Francisco riders to arrive today, big bunch coming on boat Sunday morning" and "200 expected from Stockton, 50 from Modesto and Oakdale" were but some of the immodest pronouncements carried by newspapers.

Sensing the never-ending possibilities for growth, the Wheelmen rejoiced in their affiliation with the Sacramento Motorcycle Club. A permanent union would strengthen the city's status as a racing hub. So, in early spring of 1913, at a joint meeting of the two clubs, a motion to merge came to the floor. A vote by both clubs followed. The results: overwhelmingly yes! And just like that, news flashes shot to all corners of the city, "At a banquet in the club rooms of the Capital City Wheelmen…the Sacramento Motorcycle Club…agreed to combine." All hailed the new name: the Capital City Motorcycle Club.

Four Prominent Dealers in 1913: Indian, Pope, Excelsior, DeLuxe

Since the late 1880s, bicycle shops proliferated along J and "aerial streets." Luther, Jordan, L&M Cyclery, Marston and Newbert and Landreth were but a few. In 1908, Harry R. Kiessig advertised his 513 J Street business as "The Motorcycle Experts," agent for Reading Standard and Duck. But his affiliation with motorcycles didn't last, and soon he went back to selling firearms. For a short time in 1910, William Degen & Son at 911 10th Street sold the Brush Runabout auto and the Thor motorcycle. Some sellers and transactions operated informally: one ad offered "Four Horse Power Indian Motorcycle…Call alley rear Weinstock's between 12 and 1."

By 1913, a handful of bicycle shops and other businesses carried defined motorcycle franchises. Most new models arrived by train from the factories back east. Occasionally, some arrived by steamer from Bay Area distributors. Four Sacramento dealers carried salient brands.

Cameron, the Indian Agency, 409 J: Indian, Henderson and Ace

Hiram "Holy" Cameron Jr., born in Iowa in 1891, grew up in his father's Cameron's Hardware at 409 J. Holy's mother was sixteen years old. His father, a Tahiti native who traveled the world looking for a place to put down roots, moved to Stockton in 1900 and, soon, Sacramento. By

A Capital City Tradition

Cameron (*right, in jacket*) oversaw the cart carrying a 1906 Maxwell from his Indian Agency at 4th and J. Standing in cap to the left of Cameron is rider and employee "Captain" Carter. *Center for Sacramento History.*

1908, father and son were advertising motorcycles, new and secondhand, twenty-five dollars and up. By 1910, Holy had opened a bicycle repair shop at 410 J Street. One day the show window at 409 J displayed a new sign: "The Indian Motorcycle."

In 1913, Cameron Jr. sold 104 new Indians, with 40 on order. He donated a perpetual silver cup for a perfect score in local endurance runs. In 1915, he set a record for riding 182.4 miles on one gallon of gas. More than two hundred spectators watched the young merchant on a twin Indian set this world record between Perkins and Mills. Ads boasted: "Indian Holds World's Economy Record," "Count the Indians on the Road" and "When Better Motorcycles Are Built, the Indian Will Build Them."

That same year, Cameron collided with an auto while riding his motorcycle. According to the *Pacific Motorcyclist*, he moseyed around in the park on foot, "breaking hearts instead of motorcycles. His system is to dress up and stroll around and give the girls a treat. The motorcycle goes too fast to satisfy their souls' yearnings for him."

A glass plate depicting a Native American carried the name of Cameron's Indian Agency. *Vince Martinico.*

Employee R.H. Carter, known as "Handsome Cap," made news when a hot piece of iron he was handling fell into a trough of standing oil, "causing the street to fill with smoke and tongues of flame." Multiple blasts pierced the air, causing "a miniature Fourth of July as tanks on many repair jobs exploded." Metal flew. The fire department streamed water and chemicals at the burning store. A few years later, the store would again go up in flames, thankfully stopping short of the shelf stock but obliterating the upstairs residence, leaving Cameron and his wife with only the clothes on their back.

Hiram Cameron Sr., who had brought his son to Sacramento, told the *Sacramento Union*, reported on April 22, 1917, that a man could do anything in Sacramento with seventy-five dollars. "We made it all... on J Street," he said. "My son has gone into the motorcycle business... and is prospering. He fits the business, and is not afraid of work." Son Holy must have done well, for he claimed the first seven-passenger Buick arriving by train.

Over the years, Cameron would come to be amusingly known as "Mayor of J Street." He also sold Henderson and Ace. Throughout four decades, he steadfastly supported local races by donating trophies.

A Capital City Tradition

Cameron married at least three times. In 1922, his wife Alma appeared in the July 26, 1922 *Sacramento Bee* as a figure in the business community, repairing and selling umbrella handles and frames at her husband's store. Three years later, she discovered that he bought clothes and gifts for his married girlfriend, identified by name in the newspapers. Alma promptly sought a divorce, claiming that Cameron had beaten her at their home at 2031 I Street. His second marriage lasted only three years. With third wife Evelyn, he had a son.

Toy trains fascinated Cameron. He repaired them in his shop and kept a large collection of electric cars, tracks and equipment at home. As he neared retirement, the Indian Agency turned into Cameron's Cyclery. Cameron became a charter member and secretary-treasurer of the Sacramento Yacht Club. He operated one of the first privately owned cruisers on the Sacramento River. Cameron was also a charter member off the Coast Guard Auxiliary. By now, he was living at 2832 Riverside Boulevard. He retired in 1956 and died four years later.

Kimball-Upson Sporting Goods, 609–611 K: Pope, Harley-Davidson and Cleveland

In 1891, Moses Nixon Kimball opened a bicycle shop at 705 J Street, adding partner L. Stuart Upson two years later. The shop carried athletic goods, firearms and fishing tackle, essentially assuming the legacy of former proprietor W.H. Eckhart, John Breuner's son-in-law. In 1903, Kimball-Upson moved to 609–611 K. The firm maintained a baseball team. As trends emerged, the business expanded, opening new departments: motorcycles, auto supplies, camp equipment, phonographs, radios and home appliances.

The enterprise distributed the Pope Motorcycle for Northern California. "This machine is a little demon for hills and sand…we are enclosing you an order to be shipped at once," wrote Kimball-Upson management to the Pope factory. One hundred Popes purportedly passed through the K Street business in five months, with a shipment of sixty on the way and ninety on order. The Pope rivaled Indian and Excelsior, with Harley-Davidson becoming more prominent. A glamorized Kimball-Upson catalogue listed thirteen accessories, including leggings, horns, gloves, grips and goggles. The business grew to occupy four stories, with a motorcycle and bicycle repair shop at 615 Oak Avenue.

Founding owner Moses Nixon Kimball—a descendant of the John Nixon who made the first public proclamation of the Declaration of Independence in 1776—mined gold in Alaska for several years, leaving Upson to run the day-to-day business. By 1909, Kimball returned to Sacramento for good, living with his wife at 1402 H Street. He belonged to numerous civic organizations until he died in 1945 at age eighty-two. At his funeral, former employee and by then Harley dealer Frank L. Murray served as pallbearer.

Upson lived at 715 21st Street. His roots ran deep in Sacramento. Grandfather Upson was editor of the *Sacramento Union*. Uncle Warren, Sacramento Pony Express rider, covered a perilous section of the two thousand miles over the summit of the Sierra Nevada at night and through blinding snowstorms. At some places, the trail dropped one thousand feet, with wind and snow allowing him to see only a few feet ahead.

Stu Upson, Kimball-Upson vice-president, was an early Capital City Wheelman known as a "crack rider" in his day. He wrote motorcycle competition rules and officiated at motorcycle races. Kimball, also an early Wheelman, lent a second Kimball-Upson hand at many races.

Kimball-Upson Sporting Goods vice-president L. Stuart Upson officiated at motorcycle races and led civic efforts, including the development of Del Paso Country Club. *Del Paso Country Club.*

With a sharp eye for publicity and as president of the Retail Merchants' Association, Upson helped to organize Sacramento Day in 1911 to "make the Capital City a household word in California." He was fueled by uncanny drive, even as he looked after his siblings following his parents' death. In 1910, his twenty-seven-year-old brother Burchell and a classmate at Stanford motorcycled through Europe for eight months, braving the Black Forest and down the Rhine, where other vehicles "would be of no value."

A strong supporter of the new chamber of commerce, Upson drove the effort to develop Del Paso Country Club. He served as its first president. Kimball and the firm's other executives all joined Del Paso. Hughes Stadium, the Memorial Auditorium and the Land Park Golf Course also figured among Upson's accomplishments. He was a life member of the Sacramento Rotary Club.

In 1916, a shiny new Harley appeared in the Kimball-Upson display window next to a sign, "1916 Harley-Davison is here, come and see it." The price, "$310, Pacific Coast rate—$295 plus $15 freight." *Motorcycle Illustrated* of March 2, 1916, explained the model behind the glass: "Well-known Sacramento firm signs up to handle the gray fellows and disposes of one a day." In just two months, Kimball-Upson sold eleven Harleys, some to the fire department.

In 1922, Kimball-Upson, always tuned to emerging developments, hosted Sacramento's first radio transmission of the station known as KFBK, which broadcast concerts and news bulletins. Upson's son, Lauren Jr., became an amateur champion golfer, twice winning the state intercollegiate golf championship. Stu Upson died at age seventy in 1938 and was buried at the Sacramento City Cemetery.

William A. Langley, 1015 10th Street: Excelsior, Henderson, Pierce, DeLuxe, Yale and Cleveland

Described as a merchant of bicycles and locksmith services in early Sacramento city directories, William A. Langley became a symbol of motorcycle fellowship before racing even became popular. A veteran of the Spanish-American War, he came to Sacramento from his birthplace of Massachusetts via San Joaquin County. His father, Herman, was a shoemaker and a locksmith. Records suggest that Langley joined the motorcycle business in Sacramento as early as 1907. He arranged motorcycle runs and quickly added races to his accomplishments.

Langley maintained an Excelsior racing team, encouraged by the factory. His photographs of motorcycle excursions hung outside his shop for public viewing. "Flying" Dick Galloway ran Langley's repair shop. Langley's booth at the 1911 state fair showcased a four-cylinder, two-speed Pierce Arrow and a single-cylinder machine of the same make. Excelsior's new Model 12 proved so popular that it was not available in time for Langley's exhibit.

Steady and trusted, Langley believed that the best way to sell a product was to mingle with customers. He saw the motorcycle as a means to bring people together. The back of his business card carried driving laws and ordinances. He traveled to the Bay Area to recruit "pros" for Sacramento races. When needed, he placed directional signs along a race route to

Langley (*second from right, goggles on forehead*) accompanied friends and his wife, Ellen (*far left*), outside his agency, where he posted photos of excursions to the left. Two riders held the Excelsior "X." *Vince Martincio.*

Langley's showroom featured motorcycles, bicycles, accessories and repair parts, with banners displayed on the walls. *Vince Martincio.*

A Capital City Tradition

Reindeer horns of snow garnished the handlebars of the four-cylinder Henderson, capturing the humor of Langley and his wife, Ellen, near Tahoe. *Vince Martinico.*

help riders find their way through winding courses. According to the 1913 *History of Sacramento County*, Langley earned "the confidence of the buying public...employs only skilled workmen, and his materials are good, while his charges are as reasonable as are consistent with good service and adequate profit essential to success...an admirable public spirit and helpful citizen."

In 1913, Langley sold every new Excelsior in stock. By 1914, the line had passed to Putzman & Hoffman Sporting Goods. By 1915, Langley had taken on Henderson and Pierce franchises. He moved his shop to various locations. In 1918, a new business name appeared at 725 J Street, the Sacramento Motor Supply Company, advertising "Best repairer there." The anonymous fixer was Langley himself. While carrying DeLuxe and other brands, he sponsored the Langley Bicycle Mileage Trophy Contest for the most miles ridden by bicycles.

In 1918, Langley's vivacious thirty-six-year-old wife, Ellen, featured in many of his photos, died at age thirty-six while giving birth to their first child at their home at 1521 O. The infant daughter also died. One year later, Langley married second wife Elma, twenty-three years his junior. He was forty-five. Elma accompanied her husband on many rides, just as first wife, Ellen, had done. The couple raised four daughters. Eventually, the Sacramento Motor Supply disappeared as Langley moved to new locations to focus on locksmith services and bicycle and umbrella repair. He died in 1950 at age seventy-seven and was interred at East Lawn Cemetery.

Putzman & Hoffman Sporting Goods, 1122 10th Street: DeLuxe and Excelsior

After running successful Bay Area enameling, rim, mudguard and bicycles businesses, Emil O. Putzman and Ed Hoffman opened Putzman & Hoffman, a sporting goods store, near Capitol Park in Sacramento. They positioned themselves as the "Bike Doctors." In the first three months of carrying the DeLuxe Motorcycle, thirty machines left the shop with new owners. In 1914, the business took over Excelsior from Langley.

Little is known about Hoffman, but Putzman officiated at many motorcycle races. When Hoffman dropped out of the business, Putzman partnered with others. Eventually, he formed Putzman-Bowman with fellow rider Robert Bowman. In 1917, Bowman bought out Putzman, who remained in the bike

A young E.O. Putzman (*right*), riding a DeLuxe with friends, opened Putzman & Hoffman Sporting Goods at 1122 10th Street. *Bambi Barker.*

business at 1013 J Street. Mayor Albert Elkus recruited him to serve on the Fourth of July committee.

Having served as a U.S. marine aboard the battleship *Oregon* during the Spanish-American War in 1898, Putzman chaired local Veterans of Foreign Wars and Armistice Day parades. He hosted a "bathing revue" at the Riverside Baths in Oak Park for businessmen interested in developing swimming venues. This event included contests such as best woman and best man in a bathing suit. Putzman also planned a McKinley Park carnival of horseshoes, pitching, fencing and bicycles stunts. In addition to serving as chair of the Sacramento Football League, he sponsored a youth baseball team. Wherever sports events occurred, Putzman stood behind the scenes or out front coordinating.

Putzman never married. After giving his best to Sacramento for more than two decades, the Bay Area transplant returned to San Francisco by 1940. Living at 235 O'Farrell, just off Powell Street, he found himself again involved in retail sales at a variety store. Curiously, he reported his age as three years younger on his handwritten World War I and World War II draft registration cards. He died in 1966 at age eighty-nine and was buried at the Golden Gate National Cemetery.

OTHER DEALERS, OTHER BRANDS: THOR, HARLEY, YALE, DAYTON, JEFFERSON AND OTHERS

Banta Cyclery, 825 J: Yale and Dayton

Native Sacramentan Frank Banta, born in 1889, attended Washington Elementary School. The Banta name was not new to the bicycle business. His father, Jim, had teamed with bicycle merchant L.C. Jordan in the late 1800s. By 1903, Jim Banta was listed as agent for Snell, Columbia and Monarch bikes. He also sharpened lawn mowers. Partnering with a man named Dunst, the business took on the Yale Motorcycle. After Jim's death, his widow, Laura, and son, Frank, took on the Dayton motorcycle. He employed Hardy Tompkins, a local speed king who in 1913 earned the fastest daily one-mile time at Agricultural Park on a Jefferson. Soon Banta returned to bicycles exclusively, moving farther down J Street as the city expanded. He served in the army in World War I. Afterward, he left Sacramento and worked in other towns as an elevator mechanic.

The Yale, marketed as "the gentleman's machine," was sold by Banta Cyclery on J Street. It is unknown if Frank Banta appears in this photo; William A. Langley is second from left. *Ralph Martinico.*

C.A. Fical & Son, 1926 M: Harley-Davison

An engineer who helped to form the chamber of commerce, Charles A. Fical went into the automobile business with two partners in 1910 after selling his interest in the contracting business LaTourette & Fical, the first large company in Oak Park, for $30,000. By 1913, he had added the 8 Harley to his auto lot. His ad in a 1913 motorcycle race program announced him as "agent for Harley, the greatest motorcycle ever built." In the September 13, 1913 *Sacramento Bee*, Fical ran an ad of a Harley announcing, "Fourteen of these machines on exhibit at the State Fair." His garage at 19th and M served as an official checking station in endurance races. In 1914, he advertised, "Something new on every part of the Harley"—two-speeds, collapsible foot-boards, brake and clutch control, kick starter from the pedal, full floating seat, enclosed valves, luggage carrier and spring forks. That same year, Fical moved "across street" to 2001 M, announcing that all repair work would be done by Langley's former mechanic, Dick Galloway. Soon Fical relocated to 11th and J, still selling Harley, "the fastest stock machine built." By December 1914, it likely that Harley had been taken over by J. Fink, a Stockton Harley dealer, who set up an office at 1104 J and for a short time advertised himself as Harley distributor for Sacramento and San Joaquin Counties. In 1918, son Howard Fical, an auto mechanic, traveled 44.4 miles on a 1917 twin Harley on one pint of gas, smashing the previous record earned by Indian Agency's Cameron. In 1918, Charles Fical would take over management of auto repair at Superior Garage at 1209–15 J Street. He died at age sixty in a well explosion in Yolo County.

Harrison's Cyclery, 1010 J Street: Flanders

Longtime bicycle and gun merchant William H. Harrison Jr. served as the Sacramento agent for the Flanders 4. "You'll have to hurry," urged the Flanders ads, as the bike had the "power to burn, hill climbing ability unexcelled. For $175." Born in Broderick, Harrison went into the bike repair, sporting goods and firearms business in 1901. In 1910, he began advertising his business at 1010 J, site of the former Jordan & Banta bicycle shop. In 1918, fourteen-year-old Alfred Anderson began working at the shop. While the Flanders Motorcycle didn't last, Anderson did, after buying the business when Harrison died in 1937. Anderson retired at age ninety-one in 1995, making Harrison's Cyclery arguably the longest-serving bicycle shop in Sacramento.

F.M. Jones, 914 9th Street: Kaycie, Racycle, Rambler and Flying Merkel

Agent for numerous bicycle lines and Smith Premier typewriters, Frank M. Jones carried the Racycle and the Rambler. In 1896, he advertised 1895 Ramblers, guaranteed for one year, for sixty dollars. An early Capital City Wheelman, he sold "lady's and gent's" wheels. As early as 1902, he exhibited Racycles at the State Fair Pavilion. He began taking in secondhand bicycles and advertising motorbikes. He ordered six hundred Racycles in 1910 for Sacramento and Los Angeles. While maintaining branches in Oakland, San Jose and Portland, Jones ran the state headquarters for the Kaycie motorcycle. For a time, he carried the Flying Merkel. As the motorcycle industry grew, he jumped into the accessories market with the Royal Pioneer Straps. This contraption anchored to the body, steadying an umbrella over the rider's head when rain fell. Allegedly, the outfit could be rolled and stored on the back of the cycle. By 1920, Jones was living in Oakland, where he owned a biscuit store.

Motoraid, 1113 J Street: Thor

Handling the Thor Motorcycle under the name Budd & Middlemiss, Motoraid won the distinction of being named a Federation of American Motorcyclists repair shop. In 1912, Frank Middlemiss and his mother bought from Budd the exclusive reins of Motoraid and the Thor, adding the Superior Sidecar to the inventory. Frank's brother, Thomas, served five years in San Quentin Prison for a felony described as "obtained money by false pretense." His prison mug shot showed a 1911 release. After release, Thomas traveled to Sacramento to manage Motoraid. He officiated at local motorcycle events and won sidecar races. In 1913, Thomas was again arrested on a warrant charging him with abandoning his wife. He maintained that she followed him to California from New York for "revenge." He paid $500 with the understanding that he be allowed to bring divorce action on the grounds of cruelty and desertion. Motoraid sold 150 Thors in six months. The shop kept four sidecars. By 1916, Motoraid had been bought out by Arnold & Middlemiss, eventually disappearing from the motorcycle scene. Two years later, Thomas made news when he tried his hand at inventions, fastening a twin-cylinder motorcycle to a frame to glide as an "aeroplane" with a propeller.

Sacramento Motorcycle Company and Sacramento Motorcycle Exchange, 1234 J: Jefferson

Prolific racer and hill climber "Captain" Chester Scott repaired, sold and rode four-horsepower Jeffersons, formerly known as P.E.M.s. Manager George Buell was known as "the man with the guarantee." A charter member of the Sacramento Motorcycle Club, owner Scott also started the Heelers Motorcycle Club, but decided that one club was enough, axing the Heelers. In 1910, at the age of nineteen, Scott worked for Harry Kiessig, who carried Reading Standard motorcycles. Within a few years, Scott started his own business, soon taking on the Jefferson. Ads praised the big bike: "She made the mile in…a speed of 78 mph….This motor is the Big Brother of the fast twin…of course, you don't need the Intoxicating speed with which these motors are gifted." When Sacramentan Hardy Tompkins on a Jefferson bested Oakland's Red Perkins for best-of-day one-mile time of 54.8 seconds, the Jefferson factory lauded Tompkins in ads and circulated copy, according to a 1913 edition of *Motorcycle Illustrated*: "Ask for him, [for he] knows how it feels to go 80 mph."

By 1915, the Jefferson motorcycle was dying a silent death, even as Scott picked up other brands. Nevertheless, talent didn't keep him in the business. His World War I draft registration listed him as a mechanic at the Dauch Manufacturing Company. He received an exemption from military service since his fruit farmer father had died, leaving a widowed mother. By 1930, Scott had turned to farming in Tehama County and later in the Shasta area. He came to Sacramento for a joyous reunion of the Capital City Motorcycle Club in 1948.

By the mid-1910s, it had become clear that Sacramento dealers who jumped on the motorcycle craze had a vision of an expanding industry that would revolutionize how Sacramentans traveled, spent leisure time together and participated in sports whether as spectators or participants. This vision would grow and play out over decades to come, ensuring a continued prominent role for Sacramento in the motorcycle world.

HOW SACRAMENTO BECAME A LEADER IN PREWAR MOTORCYCLE SPORTS

As motorcycles came into use by the general public, the Sacramento business climate met changing consumer needs. Garages and motor products replaced carriage yards, feed stores and blacksmith shops. One innovative entrepreneur opened Motorcycle Messenger Boy Agency on 7th Street, noted for a bike that "ran like the wind." Unfortunately, the vehicle was seized by the police due to money owed to Kimball-Upson Sporting Goods. But the demise of a good idea didn't diminish the opportunities afforded by this new mode of transportation.

As Del Paso Country Club and the Yolo causeway opened, Sacramento found itself at the precipice of an image coalescing around accessibility and style. Travel in and out of Sacramento improved. An exclusive golf club with an impressive list of members raised the city's profile. The stage was set for Cameron, Putzman, Upson and Langley to finish what they started: prove that Sacramento had what it took to assume a leadership position in the expanding sport.

Motorcycle Spirit

The new two-wheeler influenced the Sacramento lifestyle. The bikes shaped how residents spent time. Groups of both sexes mounted motorcycles and traveled together. A Sunday ride on a motorcycle conveyed status in many circles. From the earliest days, merchants sniffed out this trend

A Capital City Tradition

Afternoon outings brought out women in fancy outfits and hats and men in jackets, drawing the attention of onlookers in business suits. *Vince Martinico.*

and leveraged it in the sale of women's fashions. In the August 5, 1910 *Sacramento Bee*, the Bootery at 527 K Street used the incentive of a raffle for a free motorcycles to draw in female customers:

> *Are your SHOES different? Or just like your neighbor's? Wouldn't wear the same style of hat, would you? Let us put you into a pair of our high-grade shoes. We have the most seasonable novelties. We fit feet expertly—and guarantee satisfaction. FREE-A beautiful Motorcycle. Ask for coupon.*

Because motorcycling came with no preset mores, a perspective developed that crossed ages, jobs, education, occupation and social standing more flexibly than other trends. Motorcycles became a means for residents to express themselves as individuals, while enjoying conformity through group rides. Elk Grove, Folsom, Auburn and the Delta towns ranked high on the list of popular destinations. Some excursions followed down the coast to Pismo Beach and farther south. Langley took a group to Tijuana, an experience he captured with his Kodak Autographic Camera from McCurry's. Roads—whether paved, graveled or dirt—allowed women and girls at the handlebars to show competence roughly equivalent to men's. Kimball-Upson catalogues carried enticing drawings of motorcycles puttering in leisure along county roads. Prest-O-Lite ads

Gladys Murray on a Pope rode with a friend with a Smith Motor Wheel attached to his bicycle. *Frank and Gladys Murray Archives.*

presented idealized nighttime scenes made visible and inviting in the scope of a beam. Although newspapers reported motorcycle accidents—many driven by boys—most riders appreciated bikes for relaxed enjoyment rather than speed.

Agreeable Sacramento weather meant rides during most months of the year. A warm breeze or a blanket of stars became the perfect outing for couples, dates and friends. Women could enjoy the spring-scented air filled with blooms along the countryside. The motorcycle allowed for the exploration of routes not afforded an automobile or a bicycle. A twosome sashaying around town on a motorcycle was a way to show off a relationship or start desirable rumors.

Motorcycles gave women the independence to ride alone in safe areas, such as paths around known landmarks. Younger women in particular felt less tied to long-standing social expectations. Why walk or wait for a wagon?

A Capital City Tradition

Josephine McCarty, who married Pope and later Harley mechanic Hector Van Guelder, rode a 1912 or '13 Pope near St. Francis of Assisi Church on 26th Street. *Frank and Gladys Murray Archives.*

Dealer E.O. Putzman of Putzman & Hoffman Sporting Goods gave a ride to a friend on a DeLuxe with a skirt guard. *Bambi Barker.*

Gladys Murray, girlfriend of Kimball-Upson salesman Frank Murray, learned to ride a 1912 single-cylinder Cleveland. *Frank and Gladys Murray Archives.*

A rider in fine riding gear similar to Langley's waited at the Agricultural Park grandstand on a 1911 Excelsior Twin. *Vince Martinico.*

Women typically wore hats, gloves and skirts on a motorcycles. Ads in motorcycle magazines portrayed female riders as elegant in long leather skirts and boots with straps. When riding pants became popular, women who wore them made a statement; pants projected authority. High boots completed the look. Women enjoyed the freedom from dresses and skirts that were hot, tight, uncomfortable and cumbersome. Hats—straw, felt or knitted—rounded out an enhanced image.

Motorcycle wear for men became big business. They acquired must-have goggles, boots, shin guards and leather gloves with extra-wide cuffs splashed across magazines and brightening shop windows. Kimball-Upson Sporting Goods carried a list of fittings. The Pope factory produced ads that conveyed riders in tailored wear, often sweater and ties, portraying suitors. Similarly, ads for Cleveland and Indian projected gentlemanly young men in gloves, boots and hat, the objects of an envious public looking on. Other times, the rider was placed in settings interactive with nature, as if there were no care in the world beyond the ride.

A Fresh View of Living

Firsthand descriptions gained from the seat of a moving motorcycle brought insights into the hometown and the neighboring geographic area. Early in the century, witness accounts began to appear in magazine and newspaper editorials, articles and letters to the editor. Write-ups afforded ways to learn about Sacramento without leaving the neighborhood, such as this passage by George A. Wyman in *Pacific Motorist*:

> *Entering the splendid farming country of the Sacramento Valley, it's easy to imagine this the garden spot of the world. Magnificent farms, well-kept vineyards and a profusion of peach, pear and almond orchards....*

Concrete images gave pleasure and pride to Sacramentans who didn't know much about the local area beyond their immediate surroundings. Even a description of the Sacramento and San Joaquin Valley fog, so loathed by some, brought a sensory-based bird's-eye view rendered from a motorcycle ridden by Will S. Cluff riding a 1912 Indian from Dixon:

> *[S]o dense I could not see the road fifty feet ahead. Heavy rains had softened the road so that passing wagons cut deep ruts....I floundered through them*

without stalling. A dredger…throwing great quantities of the river bottom onto the levee.

As motorcycles penetrated daily life, they shifted from the curious to the familiar, allowing readers to examine and interpret the people who rode them in creative ways. Newspaper cartoons and caricatures poked fun at relationships. In one cartoon, a couple labored up a hill on a motorcycle, with the man steering and a heavy-set wife seated behind, not understanding the toll on the man. Another cartoon depicted a man in goggles, bent over the handlebars, trying to go as fast as he could. The woman behind him yelled, "I dropped my hair comb." The motor sputtered, *rippity, rap, bang, bang*. Not hearing over the motor, the man cried, "I don't know what you're saying, but you're right."

Sometimes humor veiled worry, as in the sketch of a hooded and winged dark "spirt" following a goggle-wearing man and woman. Titles of essays or poems made light of the risks of riding—such as "The Banshee Motorcyclist" or "The Merry Little Motorcyclist," the latter a poem by mechanic James P. Sinnot at the Service Garage at 20th and H, published in the *Bee* of September 1913:

> *The merry little motorcyclist*
> *Whirls around the track;*
> *He's always breaking something—*
> *A record neck or back!*
>
> *Success of failure's never judged*
> *By riders' feats of skill.*
> *But by the list of casualties—*
> *How many guys they kill!*
>
> *The merry little motor cyclist*
> *Leads a jolly life.*
> *He neither cares for life or limb—*
> *Who wants to be his wife?*

A Capital City Tradition

Races and Stars

The media played a significant role in fanning the excitement for races through a continuous feed of stirring descriptions. On April 27, 1913, more two-wheeled vehicles than ever gathered at Sacramento's Agricultural Park for a race sanctioned by the Western Federation of Motorcyclists. Half the races were slated for "pros" or trade riders. Newspapers talked up a track prepared with a "daily sprinkling by wagon circling the track to avoid slipping conditions" and "lime and water spread over to harden for faster speed."

Word traveled of a swelling list of competitors, with entries "pouring in" by the minute. Local boys all bore irresistible nicknames, likely bestowed by the press: "Dare Devil," "Demon," "Wild" and more. For the first time in West Coast competition, nine-horsepower DeLuxes and Daytons and twin seven-horsepower monsters were allowed to compete.

But San Francisco's Dudley Perkins, who worked in a motorcycle shop, grew annoyed upon learning that new rules required anyone working in the business to race as a "pro." This meant that he could not compete against amateurs. He reluctantly loaned his twin Excelsior to fellow San Franciscan Otto Walker.

With the best pushers in position, the frames sprang forward, ushering 3,500 spectators to their feet as they watched the Western Federation of Motorcyclist ten-mile race. Plumes more blue than brown drifted across the track. Otto Walker of San Francisco kept ahead of George Schrum, the Stockton maverick. The riders fought the back straightaway, bunching up and then again parting on the front straightaway. They seesawed back and forth in the lead. No one cared about the occasional dust rising up and mixing with scent of smoke. Finally, Walker crossed the finish line ahead of Schrum, winning the WFM Gold in 9.28.75. San Francisco's Otto Walker, riding Dud Perkins's grudgingly loaned Excelsior, grabbed the Ten-Mile Open.

As the sun moved over the grandstand, Dick Trapper, who worked at Cameron's Indian Agency and prevailed at many endurance races, earned second in a race on Jake de Rosier's old Indian "Bear Cat," said to be capable of a fifty-second mile when and "if it can be held down on turns." Local daredevil Leo McCarthy, steering a Harley, won the single-cylinder five-mile club championship.

Dudley Perkins reclaimed his Excelsior from Otto Walker to take on the three-mile Exhibition Championship. But he failed to beat the track record for the fastest mile of the day. This feat belonged to hometown boy Hardy

Tompkins on a Jefferson. Carrying Capital City Motorcycle Club colors, Tompkins triumphed to win the twin-cylinder trade twenty-miler (18:47). His fastest mile, 54.8 seconds, came on the twelfth mile. Tompkins also prevailed in the club's championship twin cycle five-mile race.

Such an accomplishment brought particular joy to the 22-year-old Tompkins. Born in Nevada County and the youngest of several children, he lived with his 100-year-old grandmother from Sonora, Mexico, on Front Street, "rear." He worked as a driver and a salesman at various motorcycle shops. In just two years, after having also dominated the miracle mile on the Bakersfield track, Tompkins would die of tuberculosis at age 24. When his grandmother died five years later at age 107, the *Sacramento Bee* speculated that she was the longest Superior, California resident, having arrived here about 1937.

But the smell of success didn't keep controversy away from the renowned Sacramento track. Six months later, tempers flared when visiting pros balked at the thought of risking their life for a paltry fifty-dollar purse. To compensate for the dropouts, the organizers scaled back the number of races. Newspapers reported that an "unruly north wind blew a gale of dust across the track…and spoiled what was scheduled." Nevertheless, a bright spot emerged: young Emil Fabian, who had surprised track officials once before, now achieving two first places and one third. Fabian would be back.

Endurance runs carried their own share of troubles. One run to Truckee, which cost twenty-five cents to enter, came with written warnings: "Don't bring a machine with open exhaust pipes" and "Don't try to have rules changed." A run to Red Bluff mandated twenty-two checking points, requiring stops at garages, shops and poolrooms along the route. On a run to Tahoe, young Fabian fell into a ditch. Langley pulled him out, later hitting a culvert and barreling ten feet over his handle bars. Pigs, sheep, dogs and a white rooster all wandered into turning wheels. Trapper won that race, earning a medal, tires from U.S. Tire and Goodyear and the Silver Loving Cup from Indian dealer Cameron.

The Capital City Motorcycle Club tendered a respite from annoying competition distractions at social activities such as Sacramento Day at the Truckee Snow and Ice Carnival, an overnight train trip. Future mayor Albert Elkus helped to plan, proving that the club still had the backing of people with influence. A printed schedule pinpointing the time of return showed an affinity for the travelers' beloved home: "5:30 a.m., Oh, you Sacramento."

A Capital City Tradition

MOTORCYCLE DAY

When the Capital City Motorcycle Club announced Motorcycle Day for April 19, 1914, a Bay Area columnist grumbled that the San Francisco Motorcycle Club alone owned the privilege of choosing the date and place for Motorcycle Day. But an emboldened Sacramento resolved to go forward. The purpose: to show the "ease of control of the modern machine and show the numerical strength of the riders."

In fact, Motorcycle Day drew clubs from around the state. Since the race program promised the first five-mile national championship in five years, the *Sacramento Union* of April 12, 1914, assured readers that a number of "crack Eastern riders are now in the South and have jumped at the chance to compete for a national championship." Three hundred machines roared into town a day early to parade down L and up K, wheels and handlebars aglow. Buttons and tags were freely distributed.

Race day dawned cool and breezy. Eight thousand people flocked to Agricultural Park. Newspapers reported, "All the throng was in good humor while the cheers echoed." Among the competitors: Tice, stock machine world record holder from Bakersfield; Perry, five-mile national champ from Illinois; Johns, Phoenix one-hundred-mile dominator from Southern California; and Balke, 1913 national champ from Illinois. Sacramento's Fabian arrived with three machines: Indian, Jefferson and Pope. Officials included Ruhstaller of the brewery business. Pixley, chief clerk of the California Board of Education, served as announcer.

Tags and buttons advertised Sacramento Motorcycle Day, April 19, 1914. *Capital City Motorcycle Club.*

But once again, Sacramento did not escape complaints when the police union decried the four-dollar-per-hour rate offered to officers to patrol the stands. The union demanded one dollar more per hour. Ignoring the feud, a few "scabbers" participated to keep "spectators from crowding into territory where injury probable." An emergency hospital corps presided. Later, the Capital City Motorcycle Club would be accused of bribing the policemen who stayed.

When the first race was announced, thirty machines rolled up to the line. They had barely fired off when Balke on an Indian shot ahead of Perry on an Excelsior in the ten-mile twin pro. As two bikes broke ahead of the rest, one roared ahead, raising the cries of the crowd until the machine fell behind, the screams only growing louder. But the rider behind soon caught the one in front. Back and forth the bikes battled, changing and re-changing positions, with Perry gaining on turns and Balke recapturing the lead on straightaways. Spectators' yells and shrieks followed the struggle until finally, on the last stretch, Balke surged for a win. But Perry recuperated soon enough, winning the five-mile twin "stripped stock" in 4:37.5 and the five-mile pro in 4:18. He also claimed the twenty-five-mile and the ten-mile free. Thomas Middlemiss, the dealer who had slept in San Quentin, won the three-mile sidecar race on a Thor.

The young, versatile Emil Fabian, who had surprised spectators and riders alike in previous races, earned first in a five-mile race on a Pope, winning the Weinstock Lubin Cup. He won second in the five-mile twin on an Indian and second on a Jefferson in the twenty-five Free. He was also known for racing on a Thor—that made four different bikes. "Boy Wonder," as he was called, belonged to the grocers of the Fabian Building at 8th and J Street. His father a musician, young Fabian was known for a gentlemanly demeanor, which seemed at odds with his ability to fearlessly enter curves obscured by dust. He handled each machine in perfect riding form by leaning his five-foot-three frame of 124 pounds left, right, forward and back. When word got out about his extraordinary wins, he was invited to join the Pope Team's "Middle West" tour. A headline blared, "Fabian to Meet Speed Demons of Nation." Fifty club members saw Fabian off. After the tour, during which he won the three-hundred-mile in Dodge City, Fabian broke track records in Woodland and beat Stockton, Fresno and other towns. In 1915, he took on Don Johns and Ray Creviston in Fresno, where he hammered them both in the ten-mile free.

A Capital City Tradition

Sway in the Sacramento Valley

While stars and races brought visibility to the Sacramento Valley, so did the number of motorcycles. With eight hundred registered in the county, the capital city reigned in the heart of the fifth-largest motorcycle state in the United States. Only New York, New Jersey, Pennsylvania and Ohio had more motorcycles. For this reason, Sacramento registered high on the gauge as probable host of future big events.

Activities of the Capital City Motorcycle Club galvanized Northern California and undoubtedly drew the attention of the national organization. Out-of-towners loved visiting the area known for dried fruit, nuts, honey and raisins. Canned goods and flour mills kept citizens employed in farming, packing, transport and sales both retail and wholesale. Members and visitors made runs to Folsom, Placerville and Log Town Hill. They navigated moonlit Delta rides and jaunts along the cotton woods along the mint-scented American River. When fourteen members rode to Reno, passing over sandy grades, an auto hit Kimball-Upson head mechanic Frank Anderson. The car was "rendered helpless," but Anderson, tough like many, shook off the shock, straightened his Pope and jumped into the seat to rejoin the competition. He earned a perfect score.

In the tradition of the Wheelmen, the Capital City Motorcycle Club knew who to include in activities that counted. The next annual train trip to the snow, "open to all who can conduct selves respectably," according to the newspapers, attracted Elks, Bankers, Freemasons and other organizations. Berths were available to the many legislators who traveled along to see ice racing on cycles whose front wheels were replaced by skates. Colfax's Hotel Gillen offered a dance during a stop on the way up.

When San Francisco's Otto Link on an Indian became the first rider in 1915 to make a round-trip ride to Tahoe, Sacramento's "Handsome Cap" Carter on a 1914 seven-horse power Indian topped him by earning first for the year on a timed 'round-the-lake trip. He steadied the bike along a melting snowline of sharp rocks and boulders. A snowdrift turned three-quarters of a mile into forty-five minutes. After eight hours and fifty-two minutes, Carter arrived home. Both feats earned center stage in a Cameron ad trumpeting "Indian Motorcycles Lead Others Follow."

As Sacramento triumphs earned the limelight, individuals ascended the hierarchy of the Federation of American Motorcyclists. Frank Woodson became state referee. Clarence Pixley, chief clerk for the California Board of Education, became Pacific Coast director. Pixley's appointment gave him the sway to advocate for the 1915 national motorcycle convention to be held in Sacramento. With arguably the best mile dirt track on the West Coast, Sacramento could be a formidable contender. At Pixley's coaxing, the city commission and other officials sent an avalanche of lobbying invitations to officials of the Federation of American Motorcyclists.

While awaiting word on selection, the club threw itself into National Motorcycle Week, May 16–22, 1915. Each day brought a focus: Sunday, Club Day; Monday, Demonstration Day; Tuesday, Commercial Day; Wednesday, Carnival Day; Thursday, Ladies Day; Friday, Bike Day; and Saturday, King of Sports Day.

THE $1,000 RACE

A race pledging big winnings enticed pros "wintering" in California after Venice and Bakersfield races to make time for Sacramento. Newspapers played the usual role of luring attendees by announcing entries of national fame, whose names were coyly announced as "in the hands of the committee,"

Emil "Dutch" Fabian was revered by locals as well as fans in Northern California towns, where he won races and established track records. *Center for Sacramento History.*

A Capital City Tradition

with "more stars expected." The *Sacramento Union* affirmed that there was not a "more thrilling sight than a closely contested motorcycle race." Custodians of the track promised "a good drench a few days before the meet," taming the dirt. Fabian, back from his Pope tour, "reeled off the mile" in fifty-four seconds in practice, expecting to chop off a second each day of practice.

Famous names, once announced, drew followers from a two-thousand-mile radius. Ray Creviston, who held the world's mile dirt track record, signed up with Perry, Balke, Walker, Burns, Artly and fearless Don Johns on a Cyclone. Fabian was back from his Pope tour, and Hardy Tompkins was rumored to have dominated the Bakersfield mile in forty-two minutes on his Jefferson. Advance courtesy tours offered visitors a chance to inspect the track for model methods to adopt back home, adding to the hometown fame. The Santa Rosa Motorcycle Club sent its entire race committee to study how the race was managed. In keeping with its elevating leadership status, the Capital City Motorcycle Club dangled a cash prize for the pro breaking the track record. The Valvoline Oil Company silver trophy sparkled in the Kimball-Upson's display window. A new time trial feature would require a one-mile solo ride without the interference of dust, smoke or competitors.

On the day of the race, nearly six thousand spectators squeezed into the stands. More oil than usual dripped from the bikes, as if bleeding anxiety. The races ran on a rigid schedule, a tactic intended to hold the animated crowd.

In the ten-mile free, Creviston on an Indian sped off in a death-defying manner, leading and clustering at the curve, until he nosed to the finish in 8:34 ahead of Perry on an Excelsior. Sacramento's Fabian seized the curves through a veil of dust that made "spectators' hearts palpitate…sometimes even the irreligious wanted to pray." He placed first in the ten-mile club championship race, second in the ten-mile pro and third in the ten-mile free-for-all, behind Creviston and Perry. In one race, Fabian slowed to allow a rider to pass him before throttling to victory. Meanwhile, Creviston nabbed the five-mile free-for-all in 4:16.

The event offered a marathon for amateurs, including one for club members north of Tehachapi. Eighteen-year-old Freddy Farwell from the Alameda Motorcycle Club swung around a curve ahead of the pack. When his Pope pedal chain broke, a moment of distraction sling-shot him into a fence. Upon recovery, an auto drove him, seated upward and smiling, to the grandstand. He waved to fans before crawling through a railing. Friends sensed something wrong. They demanded he be taken to the hospital. There Farwell slipped into unconsciousness from a fractured skull, never to awake. The May 3 *Sacramento Union* headline described the

Prominent ads brought the local public and out-of-towners into the Indian Agency at 4th and J to view gleaming new models. *From the* Sacramento Bee, *May 1, 1915.*

race as "replete with hairbreadth escapes and one fatality" and noted that "death rode at...Agricultural Park." A serious tone ran through all coverage: "Daredevil motorcycle riding punctuated w accidents and record smashing rides featured the moto races at Agricultural Park yesterday... people watching benzene bike riders flirt with funerals."

The loss of Farwell dampened the Sacramento spirit. The Capital City Motorcycle Club issued a resolution honoring the young rider. But soon enough, the town's mood improved when word came that lobbying efforts had paid off: Sacramento had been awarded the privilege of hosting the national motorcycle convention July 20–25, 1915. The event, to include two days of racing, promised an unforgettable program for "lovers of the devil wagon...distant parts of US, coming by thousands." Future mayor Albert Elkus would serve as finance coordinator.

As 700 cyclists poured into town, city leaders rolled out the carpet for 100 convention delegates at the Traveler's Hotel at 5th and J. A baggage truck accompanied the Sunset Ramble, a knot of 125 riders swelling as it progressed up from Los Angeles, picking up additional riders along the way. The chamber of commerce treated guests to moonlit river rides, theater parties, swimming at the Riverside baths and sightseeing trips by automobile to the "fruit country" of Fair Oaks, Loomis, Newcastle, Lincoln, Auburn and Penryn. Holy Cameron ran visible ads, hoping to entice visitors into his showroom.

Cross-Country Relay in Capitol Park

While 8,000 delegates mingled at the Traveler's Hotel, a much-touted coast-to-coast transcontinental motorcycle relay zoomed toward Sacramento. This spectacular feat, months in the planning, aimed to prove the potential of two-wheelers in military service. A tight schedule, starting on the East Coast, would call for 117 riders, 3 to a shift. Every ninety miles, a fresh trio would pick up the rotation, following the sun by day and continuing the westward momentum at night over five days.

The riding teams consisted of a lead rider and two backups in case the lead bike broke down. Bouncing along on the shoulder of the lead rider was a leather pouch, passed from lead to lead as each stint ended and a new one began. Tucked inside was a letter from President Woodrow Wilson to officials of the Panama–Pacific International Exposition in San Francisco. Every leg of the route appeared on a schedule assigned to a local coordinator. Sacramento's E.O. Putzman of Putzman & Hoffman Sporting Goods was appointed to manage the team in this area.

When the riders ran twenty-three hours late, Emil Fabian, assigned to ride the route from Colfax to Sacramento, backed out to prepare for an upcoming race. J. Tarbell of San Francisco was announced as his replacement.

On the afternoon of the expected arrival in Sacramento, a crowd gathered at Capitol Park. San Francisco's Dudley Perkins, the designated recipient of the arriving pouch, waited with two backup riders. As the speeding team headed toward Sacramento, the lead cycler blew a tire, calling for a backup rider to take over the lead.

Meanwhile, local boy Leo McCarthy, having participated in an earlier segment of the relay, fought rough mountainous inclines and descents on a Harley to return to Sacramento in time to compete in the upcoming race. After traveling four hundred miles day and night, he arrived too late to be accepted into the event.

Sacramento Motorcycling

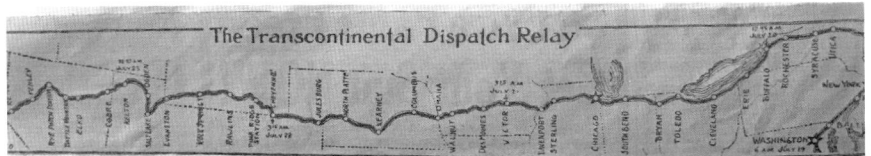

Two hundred Sacramentans awaited the rider carrying President Wilson's letter through Capitol Park in the 1915 cross-country motorcycle relay. *Capital City Motorcycle Club.*

But this didn't deter the deftly devised relay. Maneuvering some ninety minutes out of Colfax, the team came down the foothills with Sacramento in view. As the riders neared the city, fire whistles blew. Traffic ordinances froze. Members of the Capital City Motorcycle Club mounted their bikes to scour the streets for hazards.

As the lead rider burst into Sacramento at 12th Street at forty miles per hour, he crossed to 13th before an audience of two hundred people waving and cheering on M Street. There he cut through Capitol Park to hand the pouch to Perkins to continue on to the next phase. In a flash, Perkins tore out 13th to P, headed westward.

The newspapers identified the arriving rider who handed over the pouch as Heft, not Tarbell. Heft was most likely Sacramento's Schubert Ferdinand Heft, who was recorded as a "state amateur champ" and rode an Indian. Eighteen-year-old Schubert worked as an auto mechanic. His father, from Switzerland, served as the local symphony director. Schubert, after serving in the army in World War I, opened his own downtown garage. In 1925, at age twenty-eight, Schubert died suddenly, leaving a five-year-old daughter. The *Oakland Tribune* revealed, "3 Dead, 1 Dying from Bad Liquor at Sacramento. Woman and Two Men Are Poison Booze Victims." Heft and a nurse were among the poisoned. So debilitating was the effect that one of the victims fell down the stairs. The coroner suspected "canned heat" and denatured alcohol, which was not surprising, since these were the days of Prohibition. The Sacramento rider who delivered the president's message in Capital Park died a lonely death at an early age. Two decades later, a Mildred Heft—Schubert's daughter's name—signed in at a Sacramento Cyclettes' Open House, attended by motorcyclists who would have known her father. It is unknown if she ever knew the notable role that her father likely played in the historic transcontinental relay.

A Capital City Tradition

NATIONAL CONVENTION

Meanwhile, Perry, Creviston, Walker and other "motor boys" arrived in town for the awaited two-day races. Billy Leuders, twice National Amateur Champion, debarked the train from his Chicago hometown. Between practices, he visited a saloon with fellow riders. Unlike his comrades, he declined a drink. When cups were raised and tipped, a fellow rider chided, "To the Illinois kid who came to California to break his neck." Young Leuders chuckled. "I guess I will get it the same as others, but a fellow who wants to be a rider must leave liquor and tobacco alone." Everyone laughed, knowing that they were friends except when on the track.

The night before the first day of races, the usual parade made its way down J and up K. As the Golden Poppy band played, Fabian led the club division behind the Federation of American Motorcyclist officials. Tail lamps, pedals, chains and coaster brakes awarded for the best decorated cycle driven by a woman, the youngest rider, the heaviest, the tandem team coming the farthest and the largest family on a single machine—a cycle to which eight people clung "like a jitney bus."

The next morning, when the grandstand opened, billowing earth so filled the track that the *Sacramento Bee* of July 26, 1915, labeled the machines as hiding behind a cloud like "a band of sheep on a country road." Nevertheless, Johns on a Cyclone won what a newspaper termed "the prettiest event," the one-mile pro race, in 49.4 seconds. The newspapers spewed out some of the most exciting coverage imaginable:

> *Riders off to flying start…they swung around the first curve a cloud of dust poured upward, and for a few seconds only the roar of the machines gave evidence of the race…from the time the riders entered the curves until they emerged they were enveloped in clouds of dust…the sight of 10 men in a moto race sliding around the curve of a flat dirt track at the rate of 70 mph is a sight…to remain in the memory of the spectators…few if any sports before the public today requiring as great a premium in skill and daring.*

Creviston on an Indian thrashed the competition in several races. Local boy Fabian came in second in the pro race for club members. Sacramentan John Hess, on an Excelsior, claimed the five-mile amateur, the fifty-mile amateur and second in the twenty-five national amateur. Hess would go on to win the 1916 fifty-mile amateur in Columbus on an Indian. His victory appeared in a *Motorcycle Illustrated* ad, "The Wonderful Record of Bosch Magnetos," featuring the ten best achievements in 1915 and 1916.

Young Billy Leuders, the national champ from Illinois who turned down a drink and took ribbing about breaking his neck, mounted his Excelsior to win the one-mile, the five-mile and the ten-mile national amateur championships. The next day, he won the two-mile national amateur. Later in the day, as the sun moved over the track, the flag fell on the twenty-five-mile national amateur race. Leuders, knowing that this was his last race of the day, tore into the lead. One rider would later recall "dense clouds of dust dotted with ruts." Rounding the curve and flying down the back stretch, Leuders' pedal chain broke. Maneuvering with one hand to keep the chain from the wheel, he slammed into a fence. His bike sailed two hundred yards, "seemingly inspired by its owner's spirit," according to one report. Boards flew, slamming another rider into the dirt. The remaining competitors swerved around the debris, not knowing that the boy they had kidded about breaking his neck did just that.

The next morning, a newspaper mourned, "Another Racer Is Sacrificed." Agricultural Park sat quiet and deserted. The State Board of Control took a stand, forcing the Agricultural Society, responsible for the track, to ban motorcycle races. In spite of efforts mounted to allow motorcycle races, no amount of coaxing paid off for decades.

Enduring Ethos in Challenging Times

In spite of the loss of another life and the closure of the revered Agricultural Park track, motorcycles retained a fierce presence in Sacramento. As the threat of war neared, with more than nine hundred registered motorcycles here, the club kept up some semblance of normalcy, sponsoring endurance runs and hill climbs. Remnants of lingering Wheelmen rituals seeped into activities: comedy contests, whist tournaments and talks by leading businessmen. The club purchased a player piano. Members were encouraged to visit the banquet room "to be taken care of." Fred Pearl set up boxing matches at meetings.

Pearl, a Wheelman since 1890 and president when the club considered merging with the Sacramento Motorcycle Club, assumed the reins for the second time. A native Sacramentan born in 1879 and living at 1808 H Street, Pearl worked as an apprentice machinist at the Southern Pacific Shops. He held the record for riding a bike between Sacramento and Elk Gove in fifteen

A Capital City Tradition

minutes and forty-four seconds in the late 1890s. In 1914, he became manager of the fishing tackle department at Kimball-Upson Sporting Goods. He also worked at Ancil Hoffman's cigar stand at 708 K Street. Pearl loved baseball. He played center field, collected dues at Wheelmen meetings and kept time at boxing fights in the L Street Arena. In 1917, he teamed with Don Shields to promote four-round boxing. At the time, there were four boxing clubs in town. With Shields he owned the Capital Club. Shields and Pearl acted as matchmakers for all four clubs. Pearl would become a prominent boxing promoter. In his senior years, he was known to ride around town on his early high-wheeler.

A group of original Capital City Wheelmen who loved to bicycle met as Sacramento Wheelmen in a barn between J and K and 21st and 22nd Streets. Member Eugene Hepting documented many early Sacramento streets and races.

Fred Pearl, an early Wheelman and president of the Capital City Motorcycle Club, became a prominent Sacramento boxing promoter. *Capital City Motorcycle Club.*

On April 6, 1917, America entered World War I. When President Wilson announced that he was sending troops overseas, three draft registration boards flew into action. The Capital City Motorcycle Club ferried tallies and supplies throughout the county, blue flags flapping on their cycles. Of the one hundred members, fourteen enlisted or were drafted. Seven "boys" joined the Signal Corps as motorcyclists, including John Hess, who owned twelve racing medals. In 1928, at age thirty-one, Hess would be hit by a car near Chico when driving a truck for a state highway contractor. The truck split in two, burying Sacramento's national fifty-mile amateur champ under a deadly load of gravel.

With more than one-fifth of the club members in military service, those at home distracted themselves with sliding contests and barrel races. South of the M Street Bridge in West Sacramento, Carl Mankel entertained onlookers by scaling the side of a warehouse on a Harley. Gladys Murray, now Mrs. Frank Murray, won the rope jumping contest. She and Mankel competed in a "heavyweight race" for riders weighing 160 pounds. Archie Rife, mechanic at Kimball-Upson and recently elected club captain, won

Sacramento Motorcycling

Folsom Prison made for a popular destination for enthusiasts like Frank and Gladys Murray on their 1918 Pope. *Frank and Gladys Murray Archives.*

U.S. marines accompanied sidecars and horse-drawn wagons from the post office at 7th and K to deliver packages to the Mather Field Post Office in 1917. *Center for Sacramento History.*

the standing jump contest. Howard Fical on a twin-cylinder Harley clocked 44.2 miles on one pint of gas, beating Holy Cameron's old record of 92.2 on a half gallon. The annual rabbit hunt resulted in disaster, recorded by the headline, "Motorcyclists Call Off Their Banquet; Rabbits Too Tough."

In many ways, Sacramento was changing. Horses that delivered the mail were soon to retire. The Hippodrome presented a comedy, *On the Road to Frisco*, about a girl wagering that she could ride a motorcycle from Boston to San Francisco. Two teenagers on motorcycles along Folsom Road were overtaken by a band of horses, scared and stampeding from the engine noise. Both boys were knocked off their motorcycles but escaped with bruises. Joe Petrali, who would one day become a national treasure, was beginning to race and repair under the mentorship of Archie Rife.

As the holidays neared and the year 1917 came to a close, the Capital City Motorcycle Club sent greeting cards embossed with the club seal to all members in military service:

> *Just to let you know that the boys at home are with you in spirit, are proud of you and extend warmest brotherly greetings for the Yuletide.*
>
> *Capital City Motorcycle Club, Sacramento, California Xmas 1917 New Year's 1918*

LAW ENFORCEMENT

The *Rat-ta-ta-tat* that Ruled the Roads and Haunted Speeders

Three years before the Capital City Wheelmen merged with the Sacramento Motorcycle Club, the two-wheel marvel caught the attention of the Sacramento Police Department. Law enforcement already used bicycles, but the motorized bike offered speed that a bicycle did not. Criminals preyed on residential districts on the perimeter of town near 21st and T, which offered fast getaways. L Street attracted its own speeders. In 1910, Mayor Beard and Chief of Police Ahern declared an interest in purchasing two motorcycles for patrol. As the city went out to bid, a newspaper announced that the "rat-ta-ta-tat of the motorcycle would soon be heard in the still hours of the night." Harry Kiessig, who sold Reading Standard at 513 J Street, won the bid to sell the city two motorcycles at $265 apiece. The plan was for four officers in rotating shifts to share the new wheels. Four months passed as the city awaited delivery of the motorcycles from Kiessig. Finally the purchases appeared, although the model is not known—one report suggested Indian. Whatever the model, on its maiden ride, the bike ridden by Officer Reath lost a pedal, sending him into the dirt.

Within a few months, cops Harry Tharp and James Richards comprised the motorcycle duo that seemed to make news. They stopped six young motorcyclists, "mere boys" for lacking lights, fining them five dollars apiece. The officers also stopped twenty-five-year-old Adolph Teichert and two friends driving autos without lights. Teichert, who would become prominent with his gravel business, paid a twenty-dollar fine. Even

A Capital City Tradition

Police officers with bicycles surround one of their early motorcycles, thought to be a Yale, outside the temporary police department at 6th and I, circa 1911. *Center for Sacramento History.*

gubernatorial candidate Hiram W. Johnson did not escape the eyes of Tharp and Richards, who nabbed his rushing auto, driven by his twenty-two-year-old son on M Street, just weeks before the election.

Early Policing

By June 1911, Officer Ed M. Brown, who played the piccolo in the police band, had volunteered for a motorcycle beat. At age thirty-two, Brown had driven motorboats and automobiles, giving him the confidence to tackle the job. In his jacket he carried matches for lighting vehicle headlamps, which extinguished in the breeze. In later years, he described his job as calming family disputes and watching for burglars, according to the July 2, 1924 *Sacramento Bee*. The assignment that consumed the most time was chasing "reckless" speeders traveling seventeen to twenty-one miles per hour. With a speedometer that rarely functioned, Officer Brown learned to estimate violators' velocity, gauging by poles he marked along the streets. Unfortunately, his cycle's flat belt drive kept slipping, requiring him to stop every seven or eight miles to apply resin. While chasing an auto on 28th Street, his front wheel caught between the street car tracks, hurling him over the handle bars. Brown needed medical attention. The speeder escaped. One time he hit a rock, sending him into the Y Street canal. Another time his wheels skidded on a puddle, requiring two surgeries.

In 1912, the city purchased for Brown a "big, speedy" two-cylinder Excelsior, capable of seventy miles per hour. Some of the speeders Brown pursued belonged to the original Wheelmen. But savvy club leaders made a deal with Chief of Police Johnson that any motorcycle club member caught speeding could avoid jail by producing a receipt for paid-up club dues. The club would make good on the twenty-dollar bail. Not everyone was happy with this curious arrangement. One newspaper editorial slammed the police for creating a "privileged" class. Chief Johnson defended the pact, arguing that detentions had decreased among club members.

Early motorcycle policeman E.M. Brown started in 1911 on a one-cylinder model before rising through the ranks to captain. *Sally Zentner.*

Still, club members received their fair share of tickets. Three caught speeding got a tongue lashing from a traffic police judge. Clarence Pixley, chief clerk of the California Board of Education, violated the speed laws he helped to create when caught sprinting on W near 11th at forty-one miles per hour on his Harley 8. Howard Fical, fined twice for speeding to his Oak Park home, explained that he was practicing for a race. Langley the motorcycle dealer was fined thirty dollars for speeding. He was also arrested for battery against fellow rider R. Grimshaw. Allegedly, Grimshaw uttered a dig at the cycle Langley mounted outside his shop. A fistfight ensued. Langley was fined twenty dollars, but the judge found Grimshaw partly at fault.

Speeders weren't the only offenders. Harry Glover, a parks department employee who operated a sprinkler wagon at Agricultural Park, sprayed spectators at a race when national star Balke and other pros tackled the track. When the club complained, the court found Glover guilty of mischief.

By now, more than sixteen auto garages were serving the public. With the number of motorized vehicles on the rise, Sacramento formed a committee to tighten traffic laws. Clarence Pixley and dealer E.O. Putzman of Putzman

& Hoffman Goods shaped ordinances for vehicle lights and warnings to be utilized when passing another vehicle. Motorcycles were to carry a white light in front and a red in the rear, expected to shine a half hour after sunset and a half hour before dawn.

Motorcyclists assisted the police during special events. Frank Woodson, son of the early Wheelman journalist Joseph Woodson and now the city humane officer, led a motorcycle brigade deployed for crowd control. He symbolized the best of Sacramento: a man who tried to help, in spite of having lost both siblings as a young man, including a gregarious, twenty-year-old brother who drowned near Bryte. On the day before a road auto race, Woodson summoned "all motorcyclists who volunteered as flagmen and patrol men…be in City Hall this evening at 7:30 sharp to receive instruction and authority." During the race, the brigade jumped ahead of the competing automobiles to shoo cows that had broken loose with their hats and flags. When loose stringers on a bridge near Old Elk Grove were found, the brigade cobbled together cribbing just seconds before the lead car came into view.

Motorcycle merchants themselves needed police help. In the 1920s, Archie Rife's Harley Shop lost a box of platinum magneto points valued at $100. A few days later, the same register was robbed of $5, $1 stamps and $4 in pennies. Putzman lost sporting equipment. Years later, a man stole one of Frank Murray's Harleys. Al Lauer, who sold Indians in the 1930s, '40s and '50s, lost a five-hundred-pound safe, which required three men to lift. Although he was known to sleep at his shop, he was out of town on the day of the heist.

Licensing and Ticketing

From the turn of the century, California law mandated vehicle licensing for a two-dollar fee. Motorcycles needed lamps, good brakes and a bell or a horn. A curious problem arose in 1908 when the Motor Department of the California Secretary of State's office faced deciding if a buggy attached to a motorcycle was an auto, a buggy or a motorcycle when an eastern firm sought to market the vehicle here. The determination carried implications for where the license should be displayed. By all accounts, there was no decision, and the hybrid vehicle stayed out of California.

But revenue raised through fines and registration kept the local coffers more than healthy, earning Sacramento the status of the highest-benefiting

Sacramento Motorcycling

Officer Walt Greer and County Officers Robert Baker, Tom Ryan and Ed Schmidt posed outside Frank Murray's Harley Agency at 508 J Street, 1921. *Frank and Gladys Murray Archives.*

county in the state. In the early 1920s, $7,000 to 8,000 per year rolled in, thanks to fines meted out by motorcycle officer Walt Greer. By 1924, four more officers had joined the motorcycle squad. County motorcycle officers Robert Baker, Tom Ryan and Ed Schmidt brought in $100 per week.

Officer Walt Greer, riding the distinct police cycle with thicker fenders and tires, characterized enforcement as strenuous, wearing out machines in a year. Excuses given by violators speeding ranged from sprinting to the drugstore for medication to reaching the hospital in an emergency. "Boys on their dad's machine were the worst," Greer told a reporter for the May 11, 1921 *Sacramento Bee*. "I usually order them to put the machine in the police garage and walk for 30–60 days." Female drivers were also a challenge. Geer said, "They will give the speed cop [that] innocent look.... To talk up harshly, and warningly, is one of our hardest jobs."

After World War I, the number of motorcycles in the county totaled to just under a thousand, making Sacramento the ninth-largest county in the state behind Los Angeles, Alameda, Fresno, San Francisco, San Diego, Santa Clara, San Bernardino and Orange. Several Central Valley counties ran close behind, explaining the ease with which a local consortium of enthusiasts could be rallied for any event.

As expected, the number of motorcycles eventually decreased as automobile ownership increased, but this didn't impact enthusiasm. In the early 1920s, the count dipped to 420 motorcycles in the county, even as the state held its spot as the fifth-largest motorcycle state behind New York, New Jersey, Pennsylvania and Ohio. By the mid-'20s, 361 registered cycles parked in the county. In the early 1930s, Sacramento County reported only 195 registered motorcycles. Many more likely existed but were simply not registered. In fact, that year signaled the beginning of what came to be known as the "Golden Age of Racing," when speedway racing put Sacramento on the national map. In the coming decades, the number of motorcycles would rise as the population increased.

By 1956, 50,000 registered motorcycles were roaming the roads of the state, giving California continuing influence in national motorcycle dialogue. That same year, Sacramento County figures registered with the Department of Motor Vehicles approached 1,600, according to the February 27, 1957 *Sacramento Bee*.

Motorcycle Squad

At every turn, more officers were assigned to motorcycle duty, and more motorcycles were purchased. After World War I, the police department bought eleven Harleys from Kimball-Upson Sporting Goods. The preference for Harley remained, even as Indian dealers Cameron and later Al Lauer would submit bids for consideration. Most officers knew Frank Murray, owner of his own Harley agency beginning in 1919. In 1923, he sold cycles for traffic enforcement in nine counties and boasted the most complete service department on the coast. When a government official inquired about the number of miles ridden by motorcycle officers each year, Murray was identified as the go-to man for information. "The county boys all cover, on an average, 20,000 in a year's running," said Murray, an average cost of $12.40 per month per motorcycle.

Not everyone was sympathetic to motorcycle officers. When traffic officer McClellan protested the condition of his "antiquated" cycle, his superiors turned the other ear. "McClellan has had four motorcycles since he has been in the traffic department," said Chief of Police William Hilleman. "He does not need the latest equipment, as his particular duties are not to chase speeders, but to direct traffic at schools."

In fact, when two- and four-wheeled vehicles began to appear at local schools, they did not escape the watchfulness of the police department. Fritz Kaminsky, superintendent of traffic, vowed to curb wild driving near Sacramento High School. Motorcycles with cut-outs were tagged for

Sacramento Motorcycling

Members of the Traffic Squad lined up in a "V" outside the Sacramento Police Department at 813 6th Street. 1925. *Center for Sacramento History.*

Officers Frank Boniface and Frank Clayton, in a Harley VL with sidecar, marked vehicles parked too long in downtown streets. 1930s. *Center for Sacramento History.*

violating state law. Vowing to be "especially vigilant," Kaminsky met with principal and teachers. That didn't stop a sixteen-year-old arrested on K Street between 11th and 12th for riding a new "free wheeler" without knowing how to stop.

By 1928, officials were calling for every state traffic officer to patrol on a cycle, giving them the agility to whip around traffic. In one year, six more Harleys, all with radio receiving equipment, were purchased from Murray for $2,218.75. By the 1930s, a small fleet of sidecars carted officers up and down streets to mark cars "wrongly parked." The addition of "electronic warfare" of radar and two-way walkie talkies aided law enforcement. Officers waited along the road; upon getting notice of speeders, they in effect trapped them by flagging them down, saving wear and tear on their bikes. By 1958, twenty-three two-wheel motorcycles and twelve "three-wheelers" were roaming city streets.

SPEED AND NOISE

If the *s* in Sacramento stood for speeding, the *n* meant noise. In the early days, while vehicles were restricted to thirty-five miles per hour on open roads in day and thirty at night, speeds varied according to the street. Invariably, the public called motorcycles "a menace to traffic as well as to themselves." Over the next decade, traffic cases skyrocketed. P.F. Becker, traffic bureau captain, warned that "if anyone is discovered driving… if he is caught speeding on the boulevards, he will be prosecuted." Four cycle officers were redirected to intersections at "rush times" to root out speeders. By 1927, City Manager Bottorff had put more officers on cycles. Officials launched a campaign to teach traffic "manners." Frank G. Snook, chief of the state division of motor vehicles, ordered all traffic officers back on cycles, pointing out that half the squad had turned to "touring cars."

But motorcycle noise, whether from police or residents, inevitably roused the public's ire. Mayor Beard, who supported motorcycle clubs from the early days, insisted on a muffler ordinance to stop the "infernal racket." Charles Chenu, chief of motor vehicles, later declared that if laws were not enforced, his department would do it themselves. In 1927, Mayor Goddard condemned "shrilling motors that continually haunt the citizenry." A heavy fine was promised. Threats were leveled that "the Shotgun Squad out at night would be on alert." In 1928, the state passed a law that cycles had to have mufflers.

Letters to the editor printed in local newspapers clearly revealed public sentiments:

> *If anyone thinks that a youth with a motorcycle cannot [ride fast]…he should see them sometimes speeding on J, H, P, and other streets…*

> *If some poor devil over-parks his car for 15 minutes, he gets a ticket and has to pay a fine. And yet the police allow these brainless creatures to drive up and down the streets making so much noise. We cannot sleep. As I write this, they are racing up and down K Street like mad.*

> *Two cycles sped back/forth in front of hospital on J with motors wide open. City buses that stop at 40th/J seem to take fiendish delight in making as much noise in starting/stopping.*

> *Motorcycles sail through the streets gunning as far as you can hear. We have to close our door at times so we can hear TV sets. There should be a law passed to muffle these menaces.*

> *I asked what the noise was about. He said they'd come to meet chief of police of LA. I'm afraid I went home thinking about how the Germans must have felt when Hitler's Storm Troops were roving streets.*

One lone motorcycle rider spoke up:

> *The lives of cycle riders are not worth a plugged nickel anymore…now we take our lives in our hands. Car owners who dislike motorcycles try to run them down…some riders give us bad name but they are mostly youths who think they know it all.*

Ceremonial Symbol

In spite of public complaints about speeding and noise, no greater status symbol existed than the motorcycle escort. Persons of stature were flanked, preceded and tailed by officers in distinguished uniform mounted on gleaming frames. Sometimes the escorts rode many abreast and many deep. During the 1927 visit of aviator Charles Lindbergh, cycles accompanied him to Del

A Capital City Tradition

Police cycles escorted aviator Charles Lindbergh to Del Paso Country Club during his 1927 visit to Sacramento. *Del Paso Country Club.*

Paso Country Club. On the morning he planned to depart Sacramento, two hundred people jammed 12th Street outside the Hotel Senator, where cycles ringed three autos of notables amid shrieking sirens.

The annual Armistice Day parade brought cyclists guiding the grand marshal, threading around stragglers, dogs and vendors such as "King Tamale" wheeling a cart. One traffic convention opened with a parade headed by four cycles abreast, followed by the Los Angeles Police Department "crack drill team." When the Shriners met, members rode small paratrooper cycles.

When Herbert Hoover was inaugurated as president in 1929, motorcycles officers played a historic role in helping to transfer photographs to Sacramentans. Images from Washington, D.C., were telegraphed to San Francisco. An automobile rushed them to Mills Field. From there they were flown to Mather Field, where they were tossed to a *Sacramento Bee* employee accompanied by faithful officers Frank Boniface and Frank Clayton, who delivered them to the editorial room.

In the late '30s, the traffic division's fifteen-man drill team debuted at the July 4 celebration at 35th and Broadway. They gave a fifteen-minute trick riding exhibition, polished during off-duty hours in Edmonds Field and state fair parking lots. In 1942, the cycle platoon led a parade celebrating the successful war loan drive. At races held at the Sacramento Junior College stadium, the drill team's lit helmets and wheels illuminated the track.

When seventy-five thousand visitors came to town for the 1941 American Legion Convention, police formed an escort detachment that measured almost the entire length of the procession. Veterans strode down J and up K in polished helmets sparkling in the sun. Drill teams from Sacramento, Los Angeles, Fresno and Oakland performed circles. One unit split into two, turning and racing toward each other. Fearing a collision, spectators covered their eyes. At the last moment, the cycles swerved to avoid a catastrophe. "This is not what you'd call a quiet way to spend a Friday evening," called the announcer, according to the August 12, 1941 *Sacramento Bee*.

Eleven years later, at the 1952 Legionnaire Convention in Fresno, V.P. candidate Richard Nixon made news when he traveled on a motorcycle from the airport to the meeting hall, escorted by the Los Angeles Police Department motorcycle drill team.

Patrol of County Roads

In 1929, the officers patrolling county roads became members of the California Highway Patrol. At the time, there were 280 members, 225 motorcycles and 80 cars, mostly roadsters. The white motorcycle became an early emblem. "If one needs a policeman he looks for a uniform," said one observer.

By 1932, 300 CHP patrolmen had mounted motorcycles. In 1933, leg guards added protection to lower limbs. First-aid kits occupied luggage carriers, and saddle bags carried reports. Training took place at the CHP Academy at the state fairgrounds. A movie studio filmed 125 officers performing trick stunts for news reels to be flashed across U.S. movie theater screens.

One of CHP's most famous officers was Fresno native Wayne "Sprouts" Elder, international speedway star. Considered the father of American broad sliding, he helped to kick-start speedway racing here (see the chapter "Sacramento's Love Affair with Spectator Sports"). Late in his career, a traffic accident left him with a slight limp. He remained on the American Motorcycle Association Competition Committee after retiring from the CHP. But a mining venture brought legal entanglements, leading to a federal suit for thousands of dollars in unpaid taxes. Two years after his wife died, the international star loved by Sacramento ended his own life in Fresno.

A Capital City Tradition

White Harleys awaited CHP officers along the side street of Murray's J Street Harley shop in 1930. *Frank and Gladys Murray Archives.*

Blindfolded while training, CHP cadets learn to shift gears without sight, helping them balance on a moving bike. *California Highway Patrol Museum.*

In the lead-up to World War II, officers handled threats of invasion by training with steel helmets, gas masks and machine guns on their eighteen-inch wheeled Harleys. *California Highway Patrol Museum.*

In 1942, officers were trained to ride with a machine gun from a moving cycle and to use their cycle as defensive cover. By the following year, officers were equipped with gas masks, machine guns, steel helmets and tear gas guns. They learned to maneuver with a machine gun on their backs and shoot from a moving bike while traveling twenty-five miles per hour. They also learned how to use tear gas grenades.

In 1957, as helmets were issued, many officers again turned to cars, which allowed them to carry equipment such as fire extinguishers. Drivers stayed warm on cold mornings. Cars were adaptable to more shifts, such as investigation work. But over the years, some officials demanded that officers return to cycles. By 1953, the CHP had 250 motorcycles, 727 radio-equipped cars and 1,965 members.

A Capital City Tradition

THE HAZARDS OF MOTORCYCLE POLICING

With motorcycles a key part of law enforcement, the loss of officers from accidents was inevitable. In 1932, 114 injuries were reported patrolling the highways. In 1933, World War I vet and CHP officer Daroux struck the back of a car when his motorcycle brakes locked on Auburn Boulevard. The following year, CHP officer Perry hit a tree after being thrown while patrolling Fair Oaks Boulevard near the H Street Bridge when his tires blew. In 1935, World War I veteran Officer Lungershausen was hurled thirty feet, landing head first on a curb when a car hit his cycle near Stockton Boulevard and 5th Avenue. That same year, CHP officer Bond, patrolling a levee road, skidded while rounding a curve near Hood, which sent him over an embankment. In the 1940s, CHP officer Reed died while pursuing a car when a vehicle turned in front of him. In the following decade, CHP officer Hanson, negotiating a curve during training, veered to avoid an approaching car, causing him to skid in loose gravel.

In recognition of the danger to motorcycle officers, the Municipal Motorcycle Officers of California was formed in 1928 to raise funds for wounded or deceased officers and their families. In 1933, the organization sponsored one of the first flat track racing events at the new Sacramento Jr. College Stadium. Officer Bud Catlett, who participated in many motorcycle competitions, helped with grand ball fundraisers held at the Memorial Auditorium and the Eastern Star Temple. After retirement, Catlett worked on Harrah's Casino Motorcycle Collection.

SAFETY ACROSS THE DECADES

From the earliest days, law enforcement played a role in educating the public in traffic safety. Exhibits at the state fair showcased displays and demonstrations on how to approach an intersection, follow street signs and fill out a vehicle registration form. The Sacramento Police Department sponsored Safety Day and Safety Week to educate the public, including schoolchildren, about traffic safety. Women played a role in Safety Day, carrying out roles traditionally held by men (see chapter "Chrome and Polish: The Groundbreaking Sacramento Cyclettes").

In 1938, Sacramento Police Department and the CHP praised the Capital City Motorcycle Club for earning a national safety award from the American Motorcycle Association after members traveled 100,000 miles without a "chargeable" accident. At La Rosa Restaurant, the Sacramento Safety Council presented the award with the aid of Captain James Darwin of the police department's traffic bureau and CHP's Rudy Schmoke. The club repeated the win the following year, earning a fringed banner and arm bands, presented at the Espanol Restaurant, after members logged 225,000 miles without an accident, according to the *Sacramento Bee* of February 1, 1939.

By mid-century, motorcycles found themselves fully integrated into the public's traffic consciousness, if not its heart. Ordinances governing noise helped quell public ire, but the issue continued to smolder. Shell Oil sponsored a traffic safety quiz. Amid the vehicles depicted in a sketch of a highway in the May 2, 1960 *Bee*, four motorcycles weaved among trucks and autos ("Can you find 10 traffic Hazards in this picture?"). Motorcycles were here to stay. No one could doubt the existence of the *rat-ta-ta-tat* machine and the contribution of the officers who drove them.

AFTER WORLD WAR I

The Making of a Motorcycle Mecca

A fter World War I and into the 1920s, the city buzzed with visitors to the Senator Hotel, the Memorial Auditorium and William Land Park Zoo. Shoppers bustled among Penney's, Hale's and Weinstock, Lubin & Company. Everyone wanted to see F.W. Woolworth's new building at 10th and K. Breuner's advertised a "Riddance" event, selling children's motorcycles for seven dollars and scooters for five. The library stocked themed books for boys: *Tom Swift and His Motorcycle*, *Boy Scouts on Motorcycles*, *The Speedway Boys on Motorcycles* and *Bert Wilson's Twin Cylinder Racer*.

Hundreds of automobiles now traversed the roads. This trend mirrored what was going on nationally. Many people still rode a motorcycle to work. Excelsior and other motorcycle manufacturers closed, leaving Indian and Harley locked in competition, with Harley getting a leg up. Most racing programs slowed. Design work all but stopped. The national organization, operating under a different name, would eventually emerge as the American Motorcycle Association.

Surplus equipment left over from the war arrived, bringing eight sidecars for the post office for rural routes. When the Spanish flu confined motorcycle mail carriers to bed, postal officials discovered that not all substitute carriers knew how to ride a motorcycle. This lack of qualified personnel necessitated the retrieval of recently retired postal horses and delivery wagons.

Motorcycles became a delivery tool for telegraph companies, hospitals and merchant services. The Willis & Martin Drug Company at 1001 K Street kept two cycles running from 8:00 a.m. to 10:00 p.m. So familiar had motorcycles become in the minds of the public that they engendered a common understanding of time and proximity. One ad explaining the location of a plot of land for sale described the site as "an easy motorcycle run" from Sacramento.

The deep footprint of the Capital City Motorcycle Club became apparent when the *Sacramento Union* praised the club's inherited Wheelman heritage as "sturdy pioneers of time," as continuous newspaper subscribers since 1886.

When San Francisco's Cannonball Baker rolled into town on his celebrated run to Tijuana, he stopped by Cameron's Indian shop at 4th and J Street, where he was treated to Sacramento riding manners: Frank Woodson on an Excelsior and McCarthy on a Harley awaited to escort Baker through town and onto the road to Stockton, handing him off to Oakland Indian distributor Hap Alzina, who awaited to continue the ride south.

In an attempt to beat a Northern California record, members Carl Mankel and Archie Rife traveled to Stockton on a 1917 Harley sidecar. They thrashed the former mark by eleven minutes. Both Mankel and Rife would soon enter the motorcycle business: Mankel Motorcycle and Bicycle Repair Shop at 3322 Sacramento Boulevard and Archie Rife of the Harley Shop at 919 8th Street, specializing in repairs. Rife would become mentor and first employer of Joe Petrali, whose photo would one day hang in the American Motorcycle Association Museum.

Archie Rife (*left*) and Carl Mankel (*center*) reached Stockton in fifty-four minutes, smashing the previous record by eleven minutes. To the right is Frank Woodson, club president and former Federation of American Motorcyclists state referee. *From* Pacific Motorcyclist and Western Wheelman Magazine.

Indian dealer Holy Cameron, facing a slump in sales after the war, continued supplying silver cup trophies at races while pumping up his bicycle profile. He joined other dealers in a *Sacramento Bee* ad from May 10, 1924: "Be strong, robust, glad to be alive. Go places, see things, keep active. The bicycle puts the great outdoors within easy reach." Endorsing merchants included the Sacramento Bicycle Dealers Association and several motorcycle merchants who also carried bicycles to shore up their inventories.

Many Sacramento figures distinguished this era, cultivating motorcycle enthusiasts through local and regional efforts.

THE HAND THAT LIFTED HARLEY: FRANK J. MURRAY

On December 1, 1919, Frank Murray became Sacramento's first exclusive Harley dealer. The veteran Pope and Harley salesman was the right man at the right time. A swelling Harley factory paid attention to its dealers, setting the stage for an expanding presence.

Born in 1894, Murray and his elder sister, Mae, came from the Cosumnes area of Sacramento County. An employee of Kimball-Upson Sporting Goods, Murray mastered the Pope motorcycle early on, acing many endurance runs. He reported his successes to those in a position to spread the word. From a 1911 *Motorcycle and Bicycle Illustrated*:

> *The Placerville-Auburn contest. You know what a mountainous, rough country that route takes you through two forks of the American to pass. Three mountain divides to cross by Rocky Mountain roads. The little Pope was there every minute and made every grade which, I want to tell you, was an eye-opener for the rest of the boys. My riding time from Sacramento to Placerville, 47 miles, was one hour and 50 minutes....*
>
> *Yours truly, Frank Murray*

Having trained under former employer and publicity maverick Stu Upson, Murray was well suited to take over the growing brand. Setting up shop at 508 J Street, he brought credibility as a respected rider with a sizeable list of contacts.

Murray's ads emphasized factory-trained repair work and cylinder grinding. One ad in the December 23, 1926 *Bee* featured a sketch of Murray's face: "Meet Frank J. Murray…Wheel Goods of all Kinds

SACRAMENTO MOTORCYCLING

Above: Murray (*in a light cap, ninth from the right of people standing*) didn't let the Spanish flu keep him from attending a national Harley-Davidson dealers meeting in San Francisco 1919; whether or not the two women in the back were dealers is unknown. *Frank and Gladys Murray Archives.*

Opposite, top: Murray (*right*) prepared to ride with San Franciscans Dudley Perkins and Speer brothers, as well as others outside the Sacramento Bank, site of the Capital City Motorcycle Club clubhouse. *Frank and Gladys Murray Archives.*

Opposite, middle: Slow races, sponsored by Murray, tested the rider's ability to delay crossing the line. *Frank and Gladys Murray Archives.*

Opposite, bottom: Hill climbs attracted up-and-coming riders and dealers such as (*from left to right*) Gene Rhyne, "Sprouts" Elder, Dud Perkins, Finnegan Speer, Soapy Sudmeyer and an unidentified man. *Frank and Gladys Murray Archives.*

The personal quality that equipped Murray to excel was leadership. Many of the early dealers who had carried the sport to prominence were now mid- or late career. Murray, in his twenties and president of the Capital City Motorcycle Club, occupied a position that allowed him to steer the next chapter. On weekends, Murray oversaw practice runs, fast races and slow races. The latter required superhuman control of the vehicle to stay upright in slow mode, however it shook.

Murray cultivated long-term relationships with up-and-coming racers. They respected his years with Pope and Harley, carried by Kimball-Upson. Murray's business sense led him to put on races for riders who were ascending fame. Among them were San Francisco's Dudley Perkins and brothers Finnigan and Pat Speer. Murray used every opportunity to build friendships with riders, mechanics and dealers in the Bay Area and the Central Valley. These relationships would serve him when he began promoting night races at the Sacramento Motorcycle Speedways (see the chapter "Sacramento's Love Affair with Spectator Sports").

A Capital City Tradition

Sacramento Motorcycling

Goggles and leather hats signaled a 1922 endurance race to Tahoe sponsored by the Capital City Motorcycle Club; San Franciscans Finnegan and Pat Speer also participated. *Frank and Gladys Murray Archives.*

Endurance races brought out riders every time. Reno dared riders with a 325-mile round-trip, two-thirds of it mountain roads. In a race to Tahoe, riders left Sacramento in pairs beginning at 5:00 a.m. At seven thousand feet, contestants encountered raging winds. The mud ran deep from melting snow. Riders lost a point for every minute they were late and two points for every minute early. In one race, Finnegan Speer of San Francisco earned a perfect score, traveling 29 miles per hour in 12.3 hours, George Faulders, mechanic for Murray, came in second. Only two out of nineteen competitors completed the run.

The most iconic symbol of early '20s Sacramento motorcycling came in the form of Murray and his wife, Gladys, in their motorcycle and sidecar. Swaddled in warm clothes, gloves and goggles, they projected the modern sports couple. They visited the fruit country, the foothills and the Tahoe-Truckee area. They competed in sidecar and endurance races. They embraced all motorcyclists to come along, including an informal group calling itself the Sacramento Motorcycle Club. Reporter Donald Ashton covered a view from a motorcycle on one of the trips in the January 16, 1924 *Sacramento Bee*:

> [They] *romped to the majestic forest, a column of solos and sidecars headed to deep snow above Placerville.*
>
> *"Staid" cars cleared the road when the cycle columns streaked out of Sacramento....A raw, cold fog enveloped Sacramento...swallowing up objects....Automobiles swept past like ghosts...motorcycles sped along through Orangevale and Folsom until the sudden rise in the road beyond Clarksville carried them above the mist and into the glorious morning sunlight.*

A Capital City Tradition

Wrapped in warm clothes and matching goggles, Frank and Gladys Murray served as symbols of the 1920s motorcycling couple. *Frank and Gladys Murray Archives.*

Murray mechanic George Faulders, gripping his "hot rod" J model, organized Gypsy Runs, designed to bring more families into motorcycle activities. *Frank and Gladys Murray Archives.*

A run that became popular was known as the "gypsy tour," promoted by the national organization as a means to draw wives and "sweethearts" into the motorcycle lifestyle. Murray's mechanic George Faulders, trained by the Harley factory, organized such tours for Sacramento. They often involved overnight stays. In a quest to drum up enthusiasm, the national organization offered incentives such as pins. "Ladies" received monogrammed belts. When not organizing runs or repairing cycles, Faulders merited master status as a hill climber. In 1924, four thousand people watched a climb over Tarke Hill, 425 feet of ascent, a grade of 70 percent in places. In the sixty-one-inch expert class, Dud Perkins scaled 381 feet, with Faulders 354 and "Sprouts" Elder 305.

The Linked Legacy of Joe Petrali and Archie Rife

As Murray's reputation grew, two other Sacramentans etched out fame: Joe Petrali and Archie Rife.

Petrali's family came to Sacramento from San Francisco when Petrali, born in 1904, was very young. A young Petrali was said to be inspired by walking from his 5th Avenue home to watch the greats of Creviston, Johns and Balke digging into the track at Agricultural Park.

Eleven years Petrali's senior, Archie Rife, born in Illinois in 1893, came to the West Coast after his parents divorced. In high school, he played quarterback on his high school football team. At the time of World War I draft registration, he worked as a mechanic at Kimball-Upson Sporting Goods. There he repaired Popes and Harleys, equipping him with the skill to open his own repair shop. At first he advertised The Harley Shop as "successor to William A. Langley," early Excelsior dealer. Rife's ads frequently stressed helping customers to save money: "Do you know that we repair all makes of motorcycles? That we sell second-hand machines only? Harley with sidecar $200 cash, good condition."

Young Petrali visited Rife's Harley Shop daily. Barely an adolescent, Petrali quit school to work for Rife. The young man was said to be a natural mechanic. He scraped together the money to purchase a used Indian for thirty-five dollars. In time, he joined Rife at a Capital City Motorcycle Club meeting. Petrali's young hand half-sketched, half-doodled "Petrali, Historian" in the club scrapbook, leaving traces of a boy itching to jump out of the chair and fly off on his wheels. He would, in fact, soon get the

A Capital City Tradition

A young Joe Petrali, who worked for Archie Rife, drew curious onlookers as he waited on his Indian. *Frank and Gladys Murray Archives.*

chance. Although local records are sparse, interviews with Petrali recount a win in a sanctioned economy run at the state fair, traveling 176 miles on one gallon of gas with a sealed tank. This feat purportedly won him the district championship, and when the tally from all over the country was recorded, he snagged a national fuel economy championship.

Aware of Petrali's riding ability, Rife allowed him to convert an Indian single to a racing bike. Rife himself exhibited stellar performance in hill climbing. He beat Dudley Perkins at the 1920 "Vallejo Climbing Bee," as one newspaper called it. At an Auburn hill climb the following year, Rife won first place on an Indian, three hundred yards up in 12 seconds. Onlookers had never seen an Indian ascend so high and this fast. Perkins at 14.4 couldn't beat Rife's score. At the San Juan Capistrano hill climb, Rife was the only competitor besides Perkins to go over the hill, but the Sacramentan was disqualified when he swerved off course.

That same year, a unique opportunity arose when the Indian factory let Petrali ride an Indian racer prepared for "Shrimp" Burns, who had died on a track the previous week. At seventeen, Petrali purportedly fudged his age to enter the upcoming race, scheduled for Fresno. When the flag fell at that Central Valley oval, the Harley "Wrecking Crew" team boxed Petrali in. But the young genius knew a trick: making his bike pop and then looking down to feign a problem. Believing the ruse, the Harley team let down its guard. At just the right moment, Petrali roared past most of his competitors. On the last lap, he burst over the line, earning second place.

Mentor Rife shined in endurance races as well as hill climbs. He set a world record after riding seventy-seven hours in a local competition, exceeding the seventy-hour, ten-minute record. He and Joe competed in several races together. A twenty-four-hour run compelled riders to leave the chamber of commerce at 7th and H, running twelve miles along the Natomas Trestle. The purpose of the run was to see how long an engine could run. Gas and oil, when needed, filled the tanks while machines were running. Six hundred people stayed up all night outside the chamber of commerce building to witness the hourly completion of laps, totaling six hundred miles. After fifteen hours, Rife dropped out due to sickness. Petrali's Indian ran out of gas. In a similar race, both riders rode until the club stopped them after seventy-six hours. Rife came in at 1:00 a.m. and Petrali thirty-six minutes later, two days after firing up their engines.

In 1922, Rife embarked on a unique investigation. An old vault—formerly used by railroad pioneers Huntington, Hopkins, Crocker and Stanford—was located on the second floor in the main office of the Central Pacific Railroad at 54 K Street. Attempts to open the steel safe in the brick walls made any breach close to impossible. Rife and J.F. Jones, a safe expert and likely the early Racycle dealer, arrived with tools and an acetylene torch. For hours they toiled to breach the great doors. As Rife and Jones got close to dislodging the locks, reporters leaned in with cameras positioned to catch the first glimpse of a possible great fortune. At last the old doors cracked. The onlookers held their breath. The massive doors opened, creaking back on their hinges. Everyone strained to get a look. But a surprise awaited. No money, no treasure, no dazzling jewels. An absolutely empty safe!

Back at his Harley repair business, Rife began to think about changing to the Indian Company, which is exactly what he did within two years, "having purchased the entire stock of parts and machines from former agent." He added radios to his inventory. His September 15, 1923 ad announced, "Indian Motorcycle Agency, now open and still giving unexcelled service on motorcycles and bicycles." He soon moved to 1217 J Street, where he found "bigger and better facilities." But confusion arose when longtime Indian dealer Holy Cameron asserted that he himself remained the distributor for Indian motorcycles. A December 31, 1923 *Sacramento Bee* listed ads for both dealers, each calling himself distributor for Indian. Regardless of who the

A Capital City Tradition

Archie Rife, Harley Shop owner and mentor to Petrali, fought snow on a Harley J in an early 1920s hill climb. *Marnie/Archie Rife Archives.*

official dealer was, it's likely that both men saluted the arrival of the seventy-four-inch Big Chief. A contest sponsored by the Bay Area Pacific Motor Supply required enthusiasts to speculate how many parts the new model carried. The answer was purportedly revealed via telegram from the Indian factory, with prizes awarded for the closest guess. The answer remains lost to history.

By 1925, Petrali was named a starter at the newly organized American Motorcycle Association's one-hundred-mile championship in Altoona, Pennsylvania. When Joe's Indian machine failed to arrive, National Champion Ralph Hepburn offered his eight-valve Harley, proposing that winnings be shared. Petrali wasted no time in jumping into service. He got down on both knees, pulled out his tools and dismantled and then rebuilt Hepburn's motor. Jumping into the saddle, he headed for combat with Eddie Brinck, hurtling into a back-and-forth contest that averaged 100.36 miles per hour. Petrali prevailed, sealing a record for a hundred-miler that stood for years.

A few days later, a letter to Rife in Sacramento arrived from the Indian Motorcycle Company:

> *I suppose by this time you have learned that Joe Petrali won the big race. Was going to ride M-20 and in fact had already qualified on M-10. However, M-20 did not get there and in order for Joe to get his appearance money he had to ride something so he rode Hepburn's machine which blew up the day before the race. There did not seem to be a chance that this job would hang together, but it did and Joe won the thousand dollars…*
>
> *Very truly yours, TH B Carey, Manager, Parts Department Indian Motorcycle Company*

Rife knew that it was only a matter of time before his talented student would be snapped up by a factory. Sure enough, Harley management signed him to a contract. Off Petrali went, returning for occasional races. Everyone wanted a piece of Joe and his remarkable racing. He rode for Indian and Excelsior then returned to Harley, winning national titles beginning in 1926. The rest of Joe's career is well documented, making Joe a hero belonging to the nation, not just Sacramento.

By 1929, Rife closed his Indian business and joined the payroll of William Langley's Repair Shop, now at 1015 5th Street. Whether or not Cameron the original Indian dealer remained selling new models is unknown, but two years slater, a newcomer named Jim Bastin arrived from the Bay Area announcing a new Indian motorcycle and a boat business at 714 12th Street. Bastin may not have found business so good, as his agency disappeared within two years.

By 1930, with three children, Rife became a theater motion picture operator. Tragically, he faced a devastating blow when his youngest son, Robert, age twelve, died in a freak accident at home when he slipped off a ladder while playing a game. By 1937, Rife continued serving as a projectionist, Petrali put a sixty-one-cubic-inch Harley EL special racer over the 1-mile Daytona Beach course at 136.183 miles per hour, beating the previous record by two seconds. Later that day, on a forty-five-cubic-

A Capital City Tradition

A now-famous Petrali didn't let a sweater and tie keep him from trying out a Twin Flathead U at Murray's dealership during a visit in the late 1930s. *Capital City Motorcycle Club.*

inch machine, he captured the record again. His world record stood for eleven years. The same year that he won his last national hill climb, he went to work for Howard Hughes as flight engineer and sat aboard the *Spruce Goose*'s only flight.

By the time of his World War II registration, Rife was working at the News Reel Theater. He died in 1952 at age fifty-eight, after seeing his former mentee put a Sacramento stamp on motorcycle history. Rife, who served as informal mentor, would have been proud to visit the Joe Petrali exhibit at the American Motorcycle Association:

> [T]*he country's finest racer from the mid-1920s to the mid-30s, and one of the last great Class A racing stars who competed in board track racing, dirt track, speed records and hill climbs. Petrali won an amazing 49 AMA national championship races, a mark that would not be surpassed for 55 years.*

Female Enthusiasts: Riders and Spectators

Although motorcycling was open to women—in 1911 the early Sacramento Motorcycle Club welcomed female members—full participation for the female gender lagged. The sport was unquestionably male-dominated. Involvement by women was largely as observer or supporter to husbands and boyfriends. Still, some women drove their own motorcycles, rode out of town in groups and enjoyed the independence afforded by a new means of mobility. Motorcycling was a way to test gender expectations and push for choices. This women did in spite of a culture that remained relatively rigid when it came to female roles.

It is likely that some Sacramento women knew about female riders who had ridden cross-country. Some of these adventurous "explorers" may have passed through Sacramento on their cross-country rides. Effie Hotchkiss and her mother, Avis, traveled from New York to San Francisco on a Harley V-Twin with a sidecar. Augusta and Adeline Van Buren steered Indian Power Pluses cross-country to Los Angeles. Vivian Bales in the late 1920s

Wrinkled riding pants and untucked shirts showed that women rode cycles to their own picnics, held along the picturesque American River. *Magri Family Collection.*

A Capital City Tradition

Gladys Murray (*left*) and sister Irene Kaminsky attended a 1924 hill climb outside of Sacramento. *Frank and Gladys Murray Archives.*

would head this way on a five-thousand-mile solo ride on a D-series Harley. Women would have been thrilled to see a fellow female on a 1929 cover of *The Harley Davidson Enthusiast!*

In a show of determination to pursue interests, some Sacramento women drove their own bikes to hill climbs and other competitions. They traveled in riding gear, taking packed lunches. Parasols shielded those who worried about the sun. Other women participated as "accessories," hired by dealers or companies to distribute balloons and act as festive symbols. Women would, in fact, play an accessory role for decades in Sacramento motorcycling. But slowly they made strides. While there do not appear to be reliable records of local women who raced, the late 1930s brought the Sacramento Cyclettes, which marked the beginning of more meaningful involvement of women.

Significantly, women began to be seen as a distinct, emerging group of motoring consumers, even if as auto motorists, not motorcyclists. A tire company at 16th and L outlet offered to transport women to and from their personal commitments on a motorcycle while their vehicles were being worked on in the shop:

> *Firestone…1-stop service, drive in at our big, sheltered one-stop service station 16th and L, everything under 1 room, no matter how hard downpour or skittish the streets. While you are on your way to bridge or a tea—just phone…this will promptly bring one of our service motorcycles anywhere in city limits. No charge.*

The company of Wright Spark Plugs hired models to bring fun and fanfare to a hill climb near Rancho Murrieta. 1925. *Frank and Gladys Murray Archives.*

Acknowledgement of growing economic influence, however small or subtle, signaled the beginning of merchant attention to women in a nontraditional female service area.

"Zip, Speed, Sport, and Thrills"

As more women began to drive, motorcycle men in the retail community brought new models to the state fair to be seen by families. Murray of the Harley Agency and Cameron of the Indian Agency joined fellow merchants by exhibiting at the California State Fair alongside Hobrecht, Sherman Clay Piano, Heald's Business College, Fuller Paints and the Buffalo Brewing Company. Both motorcycle dealers remained active in downtown initiatives such as the "Renaissance of the West end of J,." aimed to advance Sacramento as a "first class business center" anchored by the New Sutter Theatre, the Travelers Hotel, the Sutter Club, the Hotel Ramona and the new Southern Pacific Depot.

The acceptance of motorcycles as a charming arts marketing strategy became apparent when the manager of the Liberty Theatre sent four costumed armed knights zigzagging on wheels down K Street to promote Mark Twain's *A Connecticut Yankee in King Arthur's Court.*

A Capital City Tradition

Murray brought Harleys to the general public through a 1920 state fair exhibit. *Frank and Gladys Murray Archives.*

As the country headed toward the Great Depression, motorcycles brought diversion to those who could enjoy them. Runs took riders to Napa, Calistoga and the Mother Lode. Murray displayed new Harley models outside his J Street shop. He released descriptions of new models so reporters could publicize refinements.

Frank Murray, Archie Rife and Joe Petrali, along with a handful of women, added their signatures on the motorcycle tradition started by Cameron, Langley, Woodson, Pearl, Putzman and Upson. Others would append their identities in the coming decades. As the 1920s closed out, ads described some motorcycle models as "expression of luxury" and encouraged people "Answer the call of spring…do it with a motorcycle." In spite of increasing economic woes experienced by Sacramentans, there remained no question as to the enduring truth in Frank's Murray's May 16, 1929 ad in the *Sacramento Bee*, mixing excitement with business:

> *"Zip, Speed, Sport, and Thrills—get 'em all with one of our Motorcycle Bargains."*

SACRAMENTO'S LOVE AFFAIR WITH SPECTATOR SPORTS

The "Zip, Speed, Sport, and Thrills" promised in Frank Murray's 1929 ad foretold the enthusiasm that awaited as Sacramento recovered from the Great Depression. New Deal funds brought jobs in public works projects. The Y Street levee that early motorcycle cop Ed Brown fell into was removed, and the nearby road was named Broadway. Air conditioning blew through the halls of the state capitol. The Metropolitan Airport and Frank Fat's restaurant opened. Children played with Hubley, Kilgore and Marx motorcycle toys.

Harley enjoyed a loyal following, thanks to Murray's visibility, but Indian led its own troupe of devotees. An unpleasant side to this rivalry boiled to the surface when Oakland Indian dealer Hap Alzina charged that he had submitted the low bid to sell cycles to the State of California but lost out to San Francisco's Dudley Perkins, purportedly a friend of the governor's son. Alzina testified that the state purchased only 10 Indians from him while buying 174 Harleys from Perkins. The state also bought 154 cycles from Perkins and none from Alzina, even though he bid twenty-seven dollars less per machine. The reason given: Alzina's cycles did not "meet the specs." He recounted the time the state did accept his bid, giving him the state seal for the Indian gas tanks. Upon arriving at the Massachusetts factory, he was informed that the contract had shifted to the competitor. Alzina stopped submitting bids, as he felt it was "like butting head against a stone wall."

But the good side of motorcycling eclipsed any scandal, allowing Sacramento to flourish into a premier motorcycle performance city.

A Capital City Tradition

SHOWCASE

The 1930s Sacramento Auto Show catapulted Sacramento into a trailblazer in vehicle exhibition. Held in the Memorial Auditorium, this annual show highlighted law enforcement traffic safety and courtesy tips. Frank Murray, now located at 915 12th Street after thirteen years at 5th and J, exhibited new Harley models and demountable wheels. Soon the annual auto show expanded to accessories: wheels, rims, batteries, blinker signals and headlights. The Sacramento Auto Show served as a forerunner of the famous Sacramento Autorama, which began two decades later.

THE SACRAMENTO MOTORCYCLE SPEEDWAYS

Sacramento became a flat track magnet when Frank J. Murray began sponsoring races at the Sacramento Jr. College stadium in 1933. Flat track was new to this area, but Murry knew of its success in Europe. He also knew that it had been tried in San Francisco. Murray ventured to put on a "maiden" flat track event at the stadium, where the bleachers held more than twenty thousand spectators.

Anxious to help Murray was longtime acquaintance "Sprouts" Elder. By now an international star, Elder wanted to replicate the fervor experienced in Australia and England. Named the first American Speedway champ in 1925, Elder fought the great tracks of Sydney, Brisbane, Adelaide and Perth. He also attained titles in South America. Riches came in England, where Elder commanded steep fees to perform before forty thousand people. One newspaper called Elder the greatest showman of all time.

While Elder ignited the speedway flame, Murray's formula fanned the fire by turning racing into a weekly Friday night program. He transformed the junior college stadium into Sacramento Motorcycle Speedways and himself into the managing director. When 65,588 people paid to attend, J.B. Bing Maloney, superintendent of the city recreation department, announced a gate total of more than $25,000. The city's 2 percent rental take totaled more than $5,000, exclusive of concessions. Tickets passed through Murray's shop, Lauer's Indian agency, Matt Rainey's K Street cigar shop, Paulson's pipe shop on 7th and Bowen Hardware in Oak Park. Paid attendance averaged 5,421, increasing every season. The races brought in income that football games could not. The crowd peaked on June 21, 1935, when 8,700 spectators paid. One season handed Murray a total of 97,408 attendees.

Murray's prominence in the wider Harley world and his ability to turn out the crowds earned him the influence to attract top talent. Bo Lisman, Jack Milne, Earl Farrand, Corde Milne and Peewee McCullum all signed on to chase the track. In time came Leonard Andrus, Cliff Self, Jack Cottrell, Dick Wulzen, Miny Wales, Al Chasteen, Ray (Sic Em) Tauser, Ed Koch, Bert Lewis, Manuel Trujillo, Pete Coleman and Sam Arena. The list went on because seasoned riders insisted that the Sacramento track was the best on the circuit. Wilbur Lamoreaux, or "Lammy," told a reporter that the track ranked number one among those he had ridden. Joe Petrali, now a national figure, noted that short track was gaining popularity, with riders moving up the competition ladder. A new generation of local riders became recurring competitors: Magri, Laughlin, Homer, the Tompkins brothers, Albrecht and Lauer.

Always alert to the right recipe, Murray kept the program fresh by adding novice races and dropping those that didn't excite. Among his many ingredients for what was described as "two hours of incessant excitement" were standing starts; scratch starts; match events; lap records; a, b and c classes; push or clutch getaways; and a big bike invitation. Murray invigorated the slate through team races representing Sacramento, Oakland, Stockton, Fresno and San Francisco.

Friday Night Speedway brought out the best. *Front row, from left to right*: Farrand, Chasten, Iverson, Andres, Lauer, McKinney and others. *Magri Family Collection.*

A Capital City Tradition

Al Lauer and brother Otto flanked a group preparing for a speedway run on JAPs and a CAC Harley. Between the Lauer brothers are Bill Stevens, Hector Van Guelder and Willie Woldit. *Frank and Gladys Murray Archives.*

Murray insisted on a fast, snappy program with just the right announcer. The Bay Area's Bill Meyer kept up a stream of chatter from the very second the riders rolled out of the pits. Bikes fired off like clockwork, with every job behind the scenes synchronized with precision for a rapidly moving event. The public was said to always go home "in good spirits, anxious to return."

Every season opened to a tsunami of publicity. Newspapers screamed "Flat track racing returns!" Ads dangled high drama with such prospects as: "Match Race between Sprouts Elder and Wilbur Lamoreaux, The first time these two riders have appeared together on a local track." European riders brought a "foreign threat." Newspapers promised "[t]he largest crowd ever…over 6,000 tickets have been distributed." Nail-biting coverage was assured through "all-star cards." Injuries were well covered: "Spills galore kept spectators on their feet and any riders in the dirt." Newspapers ran a who's who of injuries—Lamoreaux, Schofield, McKinney and Johnson all earned hospital stays.

Friday night races became an after-dinner social destination. Racer Armando Magri observed, "Even the Sacramento Solons baseball team knew better than to schedule their games on a Friday night. For 40 cents, you could watch a group of specialty riders from England, Australia, New Zealand and California." Magri described the thrill of race from the rider's viewpoint:

> *Speedway racers go around a very short track, broad sliding almost the entire time. Speedway bikes have no clutch, because of the short circular tracks they are designed for. You have to push start them, so the strength of a good pusher at the starting line can be important…different from racing stock motorcycles. Speedway bikes are lighter, skinnier, and more powerful.*

Wilbur "Lammy" Lamoreaux, a Sacramento favorite whom a local newspaper called "the Babe Ruth of cycling," smashed record after record at the Sacramento Motorcycle Speedways. Gene Rhyne—a multi-time National Hill climb champion who rode for Murray before becoming an Excelsior, Henderson and Indian rider—tuned a Comerford JAP bike for Lammy. They split the profits. Lammy worked for new Indian dealer Al Lauer in the late 1930s. Lammy and Rhyne would go on to win the U.S. Speedway Championship.

Murray proved to be a master at anticipating trends. He brought English, Australian and New Zealand stars to Sacramento. Murray tried the flying start with a running engine to increase speed. Eight scratch men worked the crowds into a frenzy with leans, skids and smoke. Handicapping, clutch starts and three-lap record attempts raised the stakes. A growing number of Class B and C riders forced Murray to add three novice races to each program. When top handicap riders were told to start as far back as two hundred yards, they erupted in protest—not fair and too strenuous. Yet Murray held firm, insisting that the fast guys "had to work for the win."

Murray reached outside the motorcycle sphere to try another draw: a match race between a motorcycle and a midget auto. He planned to post $500 as a bet that the two-wheeler would win. Kenneth Hupp, promoter of midget racers, agreed to the match. Lammy agreed to be the motorcyclist. Murray requested that that the race be sanctioned by the American Motorcycle Association. Hupp raised the bet to $1,000. But the sanction request failed on the grounds of danger, ending Murray's idea.

Rising in prestige in spite of a failed proposal, Murray longed for a national short track competition at the Sacramento Motorcycle Speedways, beginning in 1936. Several eastern cities wanted the race, but Sacramento's proven paid attendance at weekly races impressed the American Motorcycle Association. Murray envisioned ten thousand attendees. He imagined evening races and smaller bikes. An acute businessman, he worried when

A Capital City Tradition

Above: A trailer transported JAP bikes for Sacramento's favorite visiting racer "Lammy" (*right*), with the help of Frank Murray (*left*) and Gene Rhyne (*center*). *Frank and Gladys Murray Archives.*

Left: Ads for the Sacramento Motorcycle Speedways promised thrilling races "between the best riders in America." From *Sacramento Bee, August 5, 1937.*

top riders committed to other races when he wanted them here. He insisted that thirty "speed demons" were needed for a good competition. In the end, he realized he couldn't pull it off. Therefore, even though Sacramento was awarded the national competition, Murray declined the offer. In fact, he turned down the opportunity three times.

Pacific Coast Tourist Trophy Race

Another race held at the Sacramento Motorcycle Speedways was the Tourist Trophy, an innovative race that Murray had observed elsewhere and wanted to try in Sacramento. The "TT" model required competitors to maneuver around obstacles such as bales of hay placed on the course.

In 1939, the Sacramento Motorcycle Speedways hosted a Pacific Coast Tourist Trophy race as part of Sacramento's Golden Empire Centennial Celebration. This event came with promotional shots and publicity. The Sacramento Cyclettes, a women's motorcycle group, held a raffle to raise funds and build interest in the event (see chapter "Chrome and Polish: The Groundbreaking Sacramento Cyclettes").

Featured riders included Milton Iverson, the 1938 coast champ; Sam Arena, two-hundred-mile champion from Oakland; and Ed Kretz, Daytona Beach champion. But Sacramento's local favorite was Armando Magri. Magri led in qualifying but lost the final to Jimmie Kelly of San Pedro and instead came in fifth. Sacramentan Shorty Tompkins fractured both legs.

A 1938 Tourist Trophy showdown featured Milton Iverson (no. 19), Armando Magri (no. 2), Jack Cottrell (no. 21), Sam Arena, Leroy Kettner and Mario Stillo. *Frank and Gladys Murray Archives.*

A Capital City Tradition

A promotional shot for the 1939 Pacific Coast Tourist Trophy Championship featured Armando Magri. *Frank and Gladys Murray Archives.*

With the wave of the flag and heels off the ground, the bikes flew at the 1939 Pacific Coast Tourist Trophy Championship at the Sacramento Motorcycle Speedways, then called Sacramento Stadium (eventually Hughes Stadium). *Frank and Gladys Murray Archives.*

"You Can't Imagine the Sport of Riding Until You Try"

In 1934, a group of spirited Indian riders stepped forward to form the Fort Sutter Motorcycle Club. They welcomed riders of all makes. Founding members included Al Lauer and Joe Sarkees. They met at the Marionette Café at 12th and K Streets. By 1935, the club had more than two dozen fun-loving riders. According to one story, member Mario Bertolucci, whose son would open the renowned Bertolucci's Body and Fender, tested his Indian Scout on K Street where, on a dare, he "opened wide" until getting stopped at 9th and K. The fact that he knew the arresting cop scored not a point. Both rider and machine were thrown into a jail cell for the night. In 1936, the club became a chapter of the American Motorcycle Association. Decades later, the club joined the Antique Motorcycle Club of America and met at a house donated for meetings at 4085 Deeble Street. The club sponsored many competitive games.

Meanwhile, Murray, aware of an increasingly sluggish if not inactive Capital City Motorcycle Club, tried to attract new members through his Harley shop ads, like this one from the April 14, 1938 *Sacramento Bee*:

> *Motorcycle Sale. Join the CCMC.*
> *You can't imagine the sport of riding until you try.*

As recruits came into the club, Murray brought them together for rides and took many photos to celebrate their acivities.

Both Fort Sutter and Capital City Motorcycle Clubs attracted enthusiasts at field meets and scrambles at ranches and farm land best known by location to towns or landmarks: Glen Alder Camp, three mile north of Colfax; Roy Jackson's ranch five miles from Folsom; and the Dias Ranch near the Garden Highway Bridge. Fort Sutter Motorcycle Club sponsored games such as run and ride, hat scramble, potato race, plank jump, balloon busting, boot race, dig out race, passenger pick up, scavenger hunts, poker runs, secret time runs, English trials, turkey runs, first in show, barrel roll, Australian pursuit, stake race and steeple chase.

Equally exciting were the hill climbs, described by Armando Magri, member of both Fort Sutter and Capital City Motorcycle Club:

> *Hill climbing events were held throughout the Central Valley, including out Jackson Road. Hill climbing was a timed race up a hill…some hills were so steep, nobody could get over the top. In that case, the highest climber won.*

A Capital City Tradition

Whitie Tompkins and teammate on the Indian careened ahead of Joe Sarkees in a field meet at Del Paso Park. *Gaylene Tompkins.*

Armando Magri shows what a rider can do at the fifty-mile national in San Pedro in 1938. *Frank and Gladys Murray Archives.*

The renewed Capital City Motorcycle Club brought out both sexes for a run outside Sacramento. *Capital City Motorcycle Club.*

> *There were generally three classes; 45 cu. inches, 80 cu. inches and an open event. Special chains were put on the rear wheel, to get better traction. There was never much prize money. It was mostly for the challenge and fun. Hill climbs were a favorite with spectators Many times, the rider would loop his cycle, causing it to tumble down the hill in one direction, while the rider tumbled down on a parallel track. Crowds were well aware of the falling competitors, jumping out of the way if necessary. There were no grandstands. People just walked up and stood around.*

A Capital City Tradition

Motorcycle Polo

One of the most exciting games ever played came to Sacramento when both Capital City and Fort Sutter Motorcycle Clubs formed motorcycle polo teams. One Bay Area reporter called the game "thrills and spills from start to finish" as players "whipped around a little ball." Another reporter characterized the game as "[s]uicide polo, invented by Undertakers' Union." The teams played against the Stockton club at the Barmby Ranch, four miles east of Perkins. They also played at the Silver Spur track between the American River and North Sacramento. One time they played against the Lodi team, only to find nails scattered mysteriously around the field.

Top: The Capital City Motorcycle Club polo team lined up before getting serious on the polo field, 1937–38. *Magri Family Collection.*

Bottom: Twirling in dust with skill and precision, wheels battled one another in an electrifying polo game. *Magri Family Collection.*

Chariot Races

Hollywood slipped into Sacramento when a motion picture firm worked with Murray to stage chariot races at the 1938 state fair. A three-day rodeo would feature a trio of riders in a special event using motorcycles instead of horses. A similar idea appeared in an Associated Press photo of a chariot hooked to two motorcycles in Australia using car axles and regular wheels. Sacramento planned to do better by partnering with the movie capital of the world. News of chariots being shipped from Hollywood stoked great anticipation. Built as movie props, the wooden wheels would be "rigged up" to Harleys. Popular rider Magri and friends McKinley Johnston and Larry Hess donned purple robes and studded headbands. They steered the chariots with long metal rods. "The handlebars were braced and worked in unison," said Magri. "We could actually broad slide these things when going around corners doing 50 mph." The bikes held ground, but the wheels found little traction and slid easily. Rain caused cancelation of the third appearance. Magri admitted, "They ended up paying us $80…these machines were too bulky and powerful to mess with."

A Capital City Tradition

Opposite: In the alley by Murray's Harley shop, Armando Magri practiced steering a chariot hitched to Harleys for the special run at the California State Fair. *Capital City Motorcycle Club.*

Above: A rodeo at the state fairgrounds promised a unique race using motorcycles rather than horses tethered to Hollywood chariots. *Magri Family Collection.*

Thrill Shows and Stunt Man Extraordinaire

From the earliest days, stunt shows featured races between "man, beast, motorcycle, automobile and aeroplane" to show the relative speed of each. Motorcycles, a growing emblem of courage and danger thriving on the edge of rationality, wowed the crowds when daredevils and six-hundred-pound bears performed breathtaking stunts. Emil Pallenberg, the Shrine Circus and the Ben Ali Shrine–Polack Brothers figured among the acts that entertained Sacramentans. Riders hurled through the air at the state fair. The stadium hosted Hollywood Stunt Aces, a Cavalcade of Thrills and fiery furnaces of death. World-class performer Ewald Schnitzer climbed into a box tied to twenty sticks of dynamite set off by a detonator heard a half mile away. Shows highlighted rocket-propelled cycles, motorcycle acrobats and the "suicide twins." Local riders Al Lauer and Bud Laughlin crashed through flaming boards. In 1952, Jimmy Washburn, International Daredevil Champion, torpedoed through a burning tunnel blown up by two bombs as he reached the

A Capital City Tradition

Opposite: World-renowned stuntman Putt Mossman raced and performed many times at Frank Murray's speedway races at the stadium. *Magri Family Collection.*

Above, left: Balancing aside a full-throttled motorcycle came as second nature to Mossman, whose feats included climbing ladders, juggling eggs and shooting a gun while traveling sixty miles per hour. *Magri Family Collection.*

Above, right: A three-tiered Puttman stunt wowed the crowds every time. *Magri Family Collection.*

halfway point. In 1953, Joie Chitwood's troupe brought Harry Woolman springing ramp to ramp, over cars and doing headstands while traveling at a high speed. Children also brought novelty to the entertainment arena. "Biscuits," of North Sacramento, age seven, appeared at the Sacramento Motorcycle Speedways on a cycle built to size.

No story of Sacramento stunts can be told without the name of Putt Mossman, who competed and performed here many times. He was a talented racer who made blindfolded jumps, stood up on the seat of a motorcycle to juggle eggs on one foot, shot balloons with a pistol in one hand and a rifle in the other and climbed over a ten-foot ladder attached to the seat—all while traveling thirty miles per hour.

Born in Iowa in 1906, Mossman became a champion horseshoe pitcher at age fifteen. Known for uncanny balance and rhythm, he earned fame as an all-around athlete. He performed at rodeos, circuses, fairs, parks, stadiums, ballparks and racetracks. One night in 1935, after a bad spill with Al Lauer and Clem Mitchell at the Sacramento Motorcycle Speedways, Putt arose slowly, "holding his side and limping," but when the time came, he came riding out with his ladder ready to execute his routine.

Mossman toured all over the world, often with Peewee, billed as "the world's greatest motorcycle speedway clown," and Miss Betty Davis, a speedway rider. He maintained a $5,000 standing offer to anyone able to duplicate his feats. In addition to his stunt riding, Mossman put teams of U.S. riders together to race on the British circuit. In 1939, local riders Shorty and Whitie Tompkins caught Mossman's attention at a Sacramento race. He later wrote to them from Algiers, North Africa, where he was touring with Ewald Schnitzer, who also raced here:

> *Ewald has told me a lot about you boys and your ability to ride—and that you were both good fellows. I will no doubt need a team of six riders for the coming season in South Africa if your mother would allow you to come. I could offer you return fares and bike to ride on a percentage…you make at least $25 a week. We are entering the Sahara Desert today, 2,260 miles. Ewald and I are riding on my I.O.M. AK Supreme, 350 cc Japanese engine. We are equipped with 4 revolvers and can carry 50 liter gas 15 liter oil 20 liter water…we should make it okay. The generator is now dead, but he thinks he can fix it today. If not, we drive only by day and sleep out in the open at nights.*

Never did the Tompkins brothers join Mossman and Schnitzer, but the offer fed the dreams of the racing Tompkins siblings, who stayed in touch with Mossman over the years.

THE MAN WHO DID IT ALL: AL LAUER

If Frank Murray earned fame as the quintessential promoter and networker, Al Lauer merited a similarly high-profile reputation for excelling in more sports than most people can imagine. He claimed to be—and in most instances proved it—a racer, horseman, stuntman, race promoter, hill climber and much more for longer than four decades.

Originally from North Dakota, Lauer was born on August 15, 1907, to a mother from Russia and a father from Germany. At an early age, he purportedly became a champion hill climber for Excelsior and later a speedway champ. Lauer could be counted on to crash through a burning wall at any event.

A Capital City Tradition

Al Lauer rose in profile through racing, race promotion, a dealership and involvement in many sports. *Jerry Bland.*

An auto mechanic at local shops in the early 1930s, Lauer opened a motorcycle business at 1015 17th Street in 1934. Within a year, he was advertising new Indian motorcycles, the "Hottest Motorcycle Values in Town."

In 1935, Lauer participated in the Oakland two-hundred-miler. He raced in local and national events, often alongside brothers Otto and Fred and eventually his son. In 1938, he won the hill climb held in Los Angeles against Lindstrom of Oakland, Keller of Los Angeles and Petrali, who by then was known worldwide. Lauer sported fine equipment and, once out in front of the group, was said to be hard to catch. But he was also noted for sometimes going too fast for his own good, "spilling in the important heats." Lauer raced long after other riders his age had retired.

In 1938, Al Lauer Motorcycles moved to 923 20th Street and then later that year to 917 20th. In 1940, he employed hot rider "Lammy," the famous speedway rider.

Outside of motorcycle competitions, Lauer drove midget cars at the local stadium. He sponsored a bowling team and a war charity dog show. In 1944, he placed third in the stake race and second in Western Train competition on the horse Lady. He belonged to the Sacramento County Horsemen's Association, through which he knew Carl Selby, owner of Selby Stables. This equestrian property at Fair Oaks Boulevard and Watt Avenue became the site of motorcycle races in the 1950s between rodeos and horse shows, attended by famous cowboy couple Roy Rogers and Dale Evans.

Lauer was a founding member of Fort Sutter Motorcycle Club. His first wife, Adeline, presided over the Fort Sutter Auxiliary for several years. When her husband returned from the National Motorcycle Flat Track Races, she laid out a tabletop miniature track of four motorcycles draped in club colors of orange and green.

Thanks to Lauer, the Indian Motorcycle maintained a visible and respectable presence in Sacramento. He advertised unabashedly. When the *Sacramento Bee* printed the winners of its Kris Cringle Jingle Contest in December 1936, Lauer composed his own jingle, which he ran in an ad appearing next to the winning jingles:

> *After all is said and done,*
> *A Christmas is a lot of fun;*
> *The time to laugh/play*
> *And banish all cares away.*
> *A Stands for Al Lauer.*

Operating by his own standards, Lauer recognized women as potential buyers for the Indian motorcycle. Finding the perfect backdrop for a photo, he caught a shot of Mildred Stahlman, whose husband was an active rider.

A Capital City Tradition

Al Lauer, a champion hill climber, attacked the foothills with fury. *Gaylene Tompkins.*

Lauer's photo portrayed her not as an accessory but as a capable rider on a big bike with the prestigious California State Capitol in the background.

In the 1940s, Lauer expanded his fame by sponsoring races at area tracks up and down the Sacramento and San Joaquin Valley. Almost every night, he promoted one race or another. Some races were sanctioned by the American Motorcycle Association. Galt, one of best dirt tracks on the coast, offering a half-mile banked speedway. More than 2,500 witnesses saw Kretz, Stillo, Arena, Lammy, McDougall and Shorty Tompkins battle it out. The Lodi Grape Bowl hosted big names along with newer locals such as Cy Homer.

By 1946, Lauer had started a new weekly night program at the Sacramento Motorcycle Speedway, now called the Sacramento Stadium. He advertised, "Great sport short track racing, curtailed due to war, now back with us." Cordy, Milne, Gibbs, Lammy, Schnitzer and Ferrand leaned on their throttles before five thousand people on weekday nights. Billed as "Lauer night speedway,"

Above: Little Al Lauer Jr. held two late 1930s Indians between his hands at his dad Al's dealership at 1015 17th Street before he moved to at 917 20th Street. *Gaylene Tompkins.*

Left: Mildred Stahlman posed for Al Lauer's Indian agency on a 1939 Indian Chief, projecting women as capable as men of handling a big machine. *Tracy Stahlman.*

A Capital City Tradition

In the 1940s, Lauer promoted races around Sacramento and the San Joaquin Valley. *Capital City Motorcycle Club.*

Lauer featured inverted starts from dash events. Midget car racing shared many of his event programs. Just as Murray before him, Lauer "imported" Australian and New Zealand champ riders. In 1947, the races moved to Fridays. Lauer implemented a new plan of eight-man teams from Concord, Oakland, Fresno and Stockton. Local names included the Tompkins brothers, Paul Albrecht and Jocko Bennett. Advance publicity read, "Motorcycle skid artists will race here tonight." Ye Music Shoppe sold tickets.

Lauer continued promoting into the late 1970s with another weekly series called Al Lauer Presents Speedway Pro Class A Cal Expo Horse Arena. He brought in top Southern California speedway racers and promised extravaganzas such as "The fastest sport on two wheels." Some of these races, featuring sixty-plus riders, were sanctioned by the American Motorcycle Association. The state fair horse arena seated three thousand fans.

While Lauer was recognized for "returning Class A motorcycle racing to Sacramento," perhaps the biggest plum came in 1959, when he was named Northern California representative for the twenty-five-mile National Championship race at the California State Fair track. This signature race bought the bikes back to the oval for the first sanctioned race of its kind since 1915.

Sacramento Motorcycling

The innovative Sacramento Cyclettes, one of the first women's motorcycle groups ever, gathered for a photo in uniform in 1937. *Gaylene Tompkins.*

The first act of the Sacramento Cyclettes was to elect a president. That honor went to Gladys Murray's sister Sybil, married to Murray salesman McKinley Johnston. Sybil would serve for a dozen years. Gladys's other sister, Irene, stepped up as legal advisor. She was married to Julius Kaminsky, co-owner of Capital Radiator and Fender on 15th and F and brother to Fritz Kaminsky, chief of police. Bernadette Freitas, sister of motorcycle enthusiasts Clem and Julius Freitas, accepted the role of vice-president.

In keeping with the interests of women of the times, the club ordered skirts, sweaters, riding trousers and white blouses with a red club emblem monogrammed on the sleeve. To round out their outfits, they ordered hats. They assembled black-and-gold pins with a gold heart. The club registered with the American Motorcycle Association, receiving certification to conduct competitions.

The next order of business was to find a meeting place. The officers arranged for a down payment for a clubhouse to be built at 2319 Riverside Boulevard. The estimated cost of a structure was $1,750. Irene offered to carry the loan along with husband Julius, to be repaid as rent plus interest, of

A Capital City Tradition

The state capitol formed the perfect background for Cyclettes vice-president Bernadette Freitas, dressed in vest, gloves and cap on an early 1930s Harley. *Gaylene Tompkins.*

Sacramento Motorcycling

Handmade black-and-gold club "pins" completed the Cyclettes' outfits. *Lu Magri.*

$12.50 per month. A permit was issued for a log cabin–type design by E.E. Sydenstricker, a contractor married to Frank Murray's sister Mae.

The club's first formal activity was social and organizational: to coordinate a public card party held in the Coca-Cola plant clubroom. The officers saw value in learning to work together as a club. So successful was the card party that it became an annual affair. The Cyclettes prided themselves on their ability to operate independently, in "our own distinct and separate organization." At the same time, they asserted that "we are always [here]… to help the boys when they are putting a race or a dance."

And help they did. Soon the Cyclettes were putting on creative parties for the motorcycle boys, such as one that simulated a country fair. They arranged a Halloween costume dance. An old-fashioned Christmas party with Santa Claus followed. After perfecting their ability to coordinate events with other clubs, the Cyclettes reached out to social and civic clubs such as the Sacramento Yachtettes to help plan more affairs. Gaining confidence, members embarked on a campaign to contribute to the chamber of commerce's fund for underprivileged children and families. By saving paper and tin foil year-round, they also brought in money for the *Sacramento Bee*'s Christmas fund. They adopted a family for the holidays.

What It Meant to Be a Cyclette

Once the clubhouse was constructed and furnished, the spacious living room and adjoining kitchen became the heart of Cyclettes' organizing meetings.

A Capital City Tradition

Bernadette Freitas (*left*) and Rayma Trimble (*right*) took a spin wearing Capital City Motorcycle Club sweaters. *Magri Family Collection.*

When not planning fundraisers or taking motorcycle rides together, they hosted open houses for the Sacramento motorcycle community. These events drew up to three hundred guests for afternoon tea and conversation. The sign-in sheets reflected a who's who in Northern California racing: Albrecht, Magri, Thornton, Perkins, Cottrell, McDougall, Hector Van Guelder, Rust, Mankel, Freitas and others. The Cyclettes also attended "the boys'" races, as they called them, often preceded by dinner at President Sybil's house on Berkeley Way.

The Cyclettes developed close bonds with one another, as women of those times did. They exchanged bridal announcements, baby announcements and letters. One birthday celebration merited "flowers in white crystal candelabras, a long table covered with their unique table cloth." The printed program listed cocktails and "a toast to our friends everywhere…then dinner of tomato and cucumber salad, stuffed celery crackers, and chicken pies." When members traveled to races held out of town, they sent notes to the club leadership, opening with the salutation, "Dear Girls…" Photos conveyed their closeness, as they "signed" names over one another's faces like Mae West and Claudette Colbert, movie stars of this era.

The club held a contest awarding points to members for perfect meeting attendance and for wearing their uniform. Member Rayma Trimble reported, "Our recent AMA contest was won by Marjorie Jacobsen.…Our mileage contest was won by Mabel.…Marjorie Jacobsen placed first in the attendance contest.…Mabel Fulgham placed first in inspection, which is held monthly in full club uniform."

At the Cyclettes' first anniversary, twenty-four-year-old Myla Vance and other members gave talks on current events. As one member wrote, "Although we realize that we are a new club, we are really set to do big things in 1938." So unique was the club, and so growing in reputation, that cards arrived in envelopes addressed only to "Harley Davidson Girl Motorcycle Organization, Sacramento, California, USA."

In 1938, the Sacramento Police Department held Safety Week, representing the opportunity to contribute to traffic enforcement. Joining with the police department, at least fifteen Cyclettes turned out to help with traffic control. Four members mounted police cycles in dark skirts, white blouses and helmets. Participants were deputized by sworn oath. They wore a "regulation star," described as giving them the power of law enforcement. Duties included tagging "over-parked" cars and regulating pedestrians and motorists at heavy traffic corners. Carrying hickory batons,

Marjorie Jacobson (*left*) and Lu Magri (*right*) rode through William Land Park on a 1938 Indian Scout. *Gaylene Tompkins.*

A Capital City Tradition

Members of the Sacramento Cyclettes participated in Safety Day, memorized by a group photo outside the Sacramento Police Department. *Magri Family Collection.*

they blew whistles, directed traffic and patrolled on foot and motorcycles. They handed out good driver citations to motorists who conceded the right-of-way to pedestrians.

Although the Cyclettes were certified to hold competitive races, there is little indication they did. They did participate in motorcycle meets, such as one held in Lucerne. At the Lakeport fair, the club took second place for the best-appearing women's group. Bernadette Freitas took second in the fancy dress girl group. At a motorcycle rally in Sonora, where men's and "ladies'" stunts such as circle spinning wowed the crowd, the Cyclettes won for best group attendance, with twenty-eight members in tow. Competitions included the largest uniformed group and the best uniformed group. Bernadette Freitas won first place in the fancy riding costume contest in black "patent leather satin suit" stones, set off with a high hat, with rhinestone trim and black feathers. The following Sunday, she circled the state fair track during a sports event.

Above: Bernadette Freitas, in front of the Cyclettes' clubhouse with her 1940 Knucklehead EL, showed off her trophy for "best dressed female rider" in the 1944 Sonora run. *Center for Sacramento History.*

Opposite: The Cyclettes, including Lu Magri on her Harley (*right*), attended a 1949 field meet on their customized, "chromed up" bikes. *Lu Magri.*

A Capital City Tradition

In 1947, the Cyclettes honored their mothers at a luncheon. The program included Call to Order, roll call, introduction of guests, a poem by a member, correct usage of the American flag, a poem dedicated to dads, vocal solos, awarding special prizes to guests and a dance number by pupils of Miss Leone Arnold. The printed program carried the words to the song "God Bless America."

COMRADES LOST

While accidents occurred in the male motorcycle circles, never did the Cyclettes expect misfortune to hit their own members. Within the first few years of existence, they lost three friends. Twenty-four-year-old member Phyllis Nichols, who worked at the county Department of Social Welfare, took a riding lesson from a Capital City Motorcycle Club member. He sat behind as she handled the bike Two miles south of the Steamboat Slough Bridge, near Ryde, she lost control. The cycle crashed into a Pacific Telephone and Telegraph Company truck. He survived, but she did not.

The following year, charter member Myla Vance, who worked at the Pacific Gas and Electric Company, argued with her husband, a garage man whom she had married in secret six months earlier. The newspaper reported that she called her husband to explain that she was running late because she had been talking with a traffic policeman. Unhappy, the husband reprimanded her for speeding and brought up a traffic accident involving a child the previous year. She purportedly shot herself.

One year later, seventeen-year-old Lamar Freitas, sister of Capital City Motorcycle Club member Bud Laughlin, climbed onto the Harley of able rider Clem Freitas, her husband of eight months and brother of Cyclettes vice-president Bernadette Freitas. As the couple steered down Franklin Boulevard with Clem driving, a car hit them at Marshall Way, throwing the bride. The driver was arrested for negligent homicide. Tragedy struck again when twenty months later, Clem himself, a member of the Capital City Motorcycle Club, passed away at age twenty-five due to declining health following the accident.

More than a Fundraiser: Priscilla the Doll

In spite of the heartbreak of losing three members in three years, a beloved new project came to the Cyclettes in the form of a twenty-four-inch doll. Members named her Priscilla, the Centennial Doll. She was to be given away on Sunday, May 21, 1939, at the Golden Empire Centennial. This event was coupled with the Pacific Coast Championship, scheduled to be held at the Sacramento Stadium, previously known as the Sacramento Motorcycle Speedways. Considered an honorary Cyclette, Priscilla the doll stood over every Cyclettes meeting. Members took her measurement to make patterns for outfits. Imagining what a "well-dressed belle" might have worn one hundred years earlier, they sewed clothes for every occasion: afternoon frocks, evening gowns, wedding dress, riding habit and "old-fashioned swimming suit." Fifty-four garments rounded out her wardrobe, accompanied by fourteen hats, shoes and a tiny dog named Butch. So unique was Priscilla and her many trappings that Hale Brothers on K Street designed a display in its second-floor window. Thousands of Sacramentans viewed "the girl" with the largest wardrobe around.

After a week on display, Priscilla and her wardrobe relocated to the main floor of Hale's to encourage the sale of raffle tickets. Each day, a new outfit clothed the doll. The department store's ads in the *Sacramento Union* kept the public coming and the ticket sales brisk:

A Capital City Tradition

Priscilla the doll, shown with Cyclettes president Sybil Johnston, publicized in local media, attracted admirers to Hale's Department Store ahead of the raffle held at the 1939 Pacific Coast Championship Race. *Lu Magri.*

> *The lovely doll pictured in bridal array is a full-fledged member of Sacramento Cyclettes, Inc. Purchased by the club two months ago to dress in centennial costume, Priscilla so won the hearts of the members that great rivalry exists in the devotion offered her....Each gown is an exact copy of a fashion of the '49 era. She has 10 hats and innumerable accessories. A tiny toy dog named "Butch" is part of her walking outfit. Mrs. McKinley M. Johnston...assists at her many public appearances.*

Priscilla inspired the sale of more than 2,500 raffle tickets. On the day of the Pacific Coast race, the winning ticket was drawn. The male winner lived at 28th and E Street. The Cyclettes handed over their cherished mascot, mourning her absence for weeks to come. However, the $300 profit lightened their sadness.

From Mother Motorcycles to Mother Golf: Irene Kaminsky

Irene Chance Kaminsky, sister of Cyclettes president Sybil and Frank Murray's wife, Gladys, played a key role in the development of the Cyclettes. The sisters' mother, Mrs. Clara Chance, also attended meetings, where she was fondly referred to as "Mother Chance."

Living at 2509 V Street, Kaminsky's husband, Julius, palled around with Frank Murray. Julius's brother Fritz was a traffic officer who coincidentally signed early rider Chester Scott's World War I draft registration. A third brother, George, worked as a detective in the police department.

Irene, the eldest of the three sisters, modeled for the Cyclettes the importance of working together. She gave several speeches as part of Cyclettes' formal program (as seen in Lu Magri's scrapbook):

> *Accomplished in perfect harmony of the members. I personally believe that anything can be accomplished if the will is behind the thought....Every year that I have spent with the Cyclettes have been happy ones. Knowing that each and every one of us were as one.*

The leadership of Irene Chance Kaminsky, one of three sisters who spearheaded the Sacramento Cyclettes, left a lasting impact on Sacramento adult and youth golf programs. *Sacramento History Center.*

Irene also showed leadership through her poetry, which she readily offered at Cyclettes events. ("In harmony ten years have passed/with faith and understanding/each one more happy than the last/with frienship ever guiding"—seen in Lu Magri's scrapbook from 1947.) Members received copies of her poems, which also addressed her personal theme of the value of working together.

Kaminsky's influence spread to efforts outside the Cyclettes. For four decades, she worked as a bookkeeper for optical firms. In 1939, at age forty-five, she learned to golf after attending a driving range clinic on Auburn Boulevard, now known as Haggin Oaks Golf Course. With practice and determination, she became a consistent golfer. In 1953, she was elected to the Sacramento Golf Council, where she served as treasurer. By some accounts, she was the first female council member. Elected as a charter member of the Sacramento Women's Golf Club, she served as president for two years. She helped to organize tournaments and banquets for area golfers and became known as the "Mother of Junior Golf." Irene also lent a hand to organize a program for widows in the Elkettes.

In 1985, at the age of ninety-one, Irene died. Gladys, a life member of the American Motorcycle Association, had died the previous year. Sybil, the longtime Cyclettes president, had perished three decades earlier at age forty-eight from injuries suffered in a traffic accident in El Dorado County. None of the sisters had children. They are buried at the Odd Fellows Lawn and Mausoleum.

The motorcycle club started by the three sisters lasted fifty years, in later years attracting members such as Edith Singer, secretary to Governor Jerry Brown. No one can deny the energy and vision shown by the Sacramento Cyclettes, as well as the strides they made for future generations of women who would themselves press forward, each generation a little farther, to ride and enjoy motorcycles in a largely male-dominated sport.

BEFORE AND AFTER WORLD WAR II

Heroes of Mud, Skies and Track

While "Frenesi" by Artie Shaw and "I'll Never Smile Again" by Tommy Dorsey played on the Zenith console at the Cyclettes' clubhouse, M Street became Capitol Avenue and an open-air mall named Town and Country Village drew shoppers to Fulton and Marconi. Newspapers ran ads for delivery services: "Girl motorcycle rider wanted," or "Motorcycle boy or girl for pickup/delivery service apply service dept. Spencer Elliott Co. 1700 K."

Frank Murray gave up weekly speedway races after promising "[t]he fastest motorcycle racers in the world." References to riders "cutting each other's throats" failed to gain traction. Gas rationing lingered on the horizon. A tax on sports events would require a raise in admission fees from forty to forty-five cents. Even if these factors didn't exist, top riders were bound to race commitments elsewhere, preventing them from coming to Sacramento. No amount of clutch starts or grudge matches touted by Murray could re-create his Sacramento "Golden Age of Racing." Within a decade, British bikes would invade Sacramento, bringing a new wave of racing that was surging in Europe, such as motocross.

As the nation prepared for war, the call went out in 1940 for men ages twenty-one to forty-five to register for the draft, recruiters set up stations at the Stoll Building at 5th and K and the Federal Building at 7th and K. On Registration Day, eighteen Capital City Motorcycle Club volunteers ferried tallies and supplies, zipping through the county, blue flags waving from the tails of their bikes.

A Capital City Tradition

With the worry of war, the American Motorcycle Association canceled most championship races. News came that Stockton's Field Helguson, who had torn up the track here many times, died over the English Channel while serving in the Royal Air Force. The U.S. Army had turned him down because of fingers he had lost in a motorcycle race.

But in spite of tragedies prewar and postwar, this period would deliver many outstanding Sacramento racers and activities whose names would endure.

SHOWMAN ON WHEELS: ARMANDO MAGRI

Armando Magri, who would become Sacramento's second exclusive new Harley dealer after Frank Murray retired, carved a legendary racing career. He was a rider's rider: a man who would jump on a motorcycle and ride to compete anywhere, anytime. His passion was complemented by his personality. He was a master of amusement. While other riders grew impatient waiting for a run to begin, Magri diffused boredom with humor and a smile.

Born in Chico in 1914, Magri and his elder brother Ernie learned to ride as young teens on a 1921 Harley WJ Sport Twin, taught by a nineteen-year-old female neighbor. In 1936, Armando moved to Sacramento after having won some races and catching the attention of Murray, who signed him on as a Class C rider, competing with the likes of Ed Kretz, Jack Cottrell, Sam Arena and Mario Stillo. Magri entered any race he could, and the local newspapers kept the public up on his successes, including a win at the Saugus TT in 1937. In 1938, at the National Miniature Tourist Trophy Championship in Marion, Indiana, Magri won his heat on a Harley Knucklehead that he had ridden there. When he accidentally started the main event with his bike in neutral, he compensated by flying like crazy the entire race, finishing third. At this event, he met Walter Davidson Jr., son of the Harley cofounder, who would become a lifelong friend.

In 1939, the dashing Armando married girlfriend Lu, active in the Sacramento Cyclettes. On the day they married, the Capital City Motorcycle Club drill team—elegant in black breeches, boots and shirts; white belts and ties; and chrome helmets—escorted the newlyweds from the church to the reception. At the 1939 Pacific Coast Championship, at Sacramento Stadium, Magri won the pole position but could not win the main event in his adopted town. Jimmy Kelly won on an Indian. Also in 1939, at the Oakland two-

Left: With helmet and goggles at his foot, Armando Magri reviewed the race program with some of the best who raced here: Sam Arena, Bill Pond and Jack Cottrell. 1939. *Frank and Gladys Murray Archives.*

Below: Magri showed the Stockton track that he could master the challenge on his Harley WLDR in 1941. *Magri Family Collection.*

A Capital City Tradition

hundred-mile national, he was awarded second behind Jack Cottrell. But several observers protested that the laps had been miscounted and argued that Magri was the first to cross the line. Unfortunately, officials had already announced the winner and given the trophy and prize money to Cottrell, and they would not comply with the request. Magri's luck turned around when he won the 1941 50-mile Pacific Coast Tourist Trophy Championship at Bolado Park, just outside of Hollister.

Hoping to become a motorcycle instructor as the country prepared for war, Magri jumped on his Harley and headed to Fort Knox, Kentucky, at the suggestion of a member of the Harley family. When he arrived, he learned that the job he expected was not to be. Eventually, he worked his way into a role that enabled him to teach and race against men of higher rank. One special event was 1943's second annual Fort Knox Endurance Run, sponsored by the army motorcycle school.

As Magri described:

> *Every running motorcycle at the fort was entered, 105 in all, and 25 more turned away. We took off in 60 second intervals. I was riding a 1942 Harley WLA 45 cubic inch model, made for the U.S. Army (thus, the designation "A"). There were also a couple of XA Harleys. These were shaft-drive BMW facsimiles that the Harley manufactured for Army use in North Africa.*
>
> *The course was a mass of mud and clay....While other guys got stuck trying to plow through mud, I stayed in the high spots in-between. Fencepost were a bit higher too, so I rode as close as I could. I kept a lookout for clean water puddles that would wash mud off the wheels....One entrant told the H-D Enthusiast magazine photographer "This is just a picnic," before he encountered the worst of the mud...competitors didn't understand their motorcycles enough; that you can't let that much mud get between the wheels and fenders. Their bikes sunk down into the mud so badly that they couldn't get unstuck....Only six of us finished within the allotted time.*

After the war, Magri placed fourth in the 1948 one-hundred-mile Riverside Tourist Trophy. In 1950, he and Lu bought Frank Murray's Harley dealership. Magri maintained a visible role in the motorcycling community for decades. He was a "motorcyclist's motorcyclist," up for every call. When KCRA needed help at the start of the 1960 Summer Olympics, they knew who they could call (see the section "The Coldest Ride: Race to Olympic Village").

U.S. Army contestants on Harley 45s got ready for the endurance run at Fort Knox. *Magri Family Collection.*

In retirement, Magri restored a 1936 EL Knucklehead, a 1950 FL pinhead sidecar, a military XA, a replica of his old WLDR racing machine and a 1921 WJ Sport Twin. He swung on a motorcycle until age eighty-six, loving every minute.

Famous Flying Triple Ace: Cyril Homer

Born in 1919 and grandson of state senator Joseph Adams Filcher, Cy Homer attended San Juan High School. According to his family, he may have suffered polio as a child, which left him with a slight limp. He took classes at Sacramento Junior College. A superior broad slider, he worked for San Francisco dealer Hap Jones. A race left him with jaw injuries. He enlisted in the Army Reserves and was later accepted into U.S. Army Air Corps flight training. Some say he had difficulty fitting on the oxygen mask due to his jaw injuries. He overcame this challenge and learned to fly a P-38

A Capital City Tradition

Sacramento's Flying Triple Ace Cy Homer (*right*), here with Chico's Mario Stillo, called motorcycles "tame" compared to war. *Cy Homer Collection.*

plane. According to records, some hardened military officials looked askance at the new pilot with physical imperfections. Their reservations vanished the minute they saw his extraordinary flight maneuvers.

Sent to Australia, Homer's first major mission came in 1942, strafing aircraft over Dutch New Guinea with occasional offensive operations. Comrades considered him the best flier of the squadron. Homer dubbed his Lightning "Yank from Hell." His other planes carried the inscription "Uncle Cy's Angel." In time, Homer took command of his flying group, a role he kept until May 1945. He shot down enemy planes. His squadron pounded air strips and harbor alike with four hundred tons of bombs. More than once, adversary planes blanketed the sky. Once, he destroyed four planes, his highest score for a single raid. Twice he shot down three planes on a single run. He pursued three enemy planes and shot down one, only to sight two enemy fighters attacking. He engaged them and destroyed both. When he spotted more planes about to attack, he turned directly into them, taking on full force. But Homer managed to elude fire and aided another pilot under attack. With anti-aircraft fire striking around him and his damaged plane low on fuel, he pursued the enemy for several minutes before being forced to return.

Later, Homer would recount one single night when he lost twenty-three planes in a bombing raid. "We'd fly right over and strafe their strips. We left 21 planes burning on the ground at Fabrica." On many occasions, Homer returned with only one motor.

In the Philippines in December 1944, Homer flew against the Japanese island of Kyushu. His Lightnings strafed the Japanese naval force for three hours, halting ships until bombers came from distant bases. Despite the fact that the group did not have time to load bombs and used only small-caliber bullets, they sunk a ship. On the day of surrender, the squadron shot down its last enemy plane.

Homer's group earned two Distinguished Unit Citations. In nine campaigns, the group shot down 446 aircraft, creating twenty-four flying aces, including Homer. According to his family and unofficial records, he actually downed 18 Japanese planes, but only 15 were formally confirmed.

After the war, Homer was sought out for many interviews. The public and military writers alike wanted to talk with Sacramento's Triple Ace. Homer and his successes are recounted in several books. Once—noted in *"Twelve to One" V Fighter Command Aces of the Pacific*, compiled by Tony Holmes—he gave out his rules for combat flying, some of which he may have used during motorcycle races:

Cy Homer's Rules for Combat Flying

Always clear your tail before firing.
Always try to use the element of surprise.
Always close in, and then use short bursts.
Always take advantage of sun and cloud cover.
Always hit the enemy when they are thickest.
Always try to join with another friendly airplane.

Sacramento's Triple Ace received the Air Medal (nine oak leaf cluster), Asiatic Pacific Campaign Medal, World War II Victory Medal, the Silver Star and three Distinguished Flying Crosses with oak leaf clusters and six battle stars. He was quoted as wanting to return to motorcycles when out of uniform, although he found riding "tame in some respects."

Returning home, he won many motorcycle races and was considered one of Sacramento's best. According to the July 8, 1945 *Sacramento Bee*, he was once stopped by a CHP officer who had noticed that the license hung from the side of his motorcycle fender instead of the back. The officer admonished the rider, only to realize that he stood face to face with Sacramento's top fighter ace, "who had 18 personal citations, three distinguished flying crosses, nine air medals, downed 18 Jap planes in 238 combat missions." Upon realizing, the officer purportedly waved Homer on.

After working as a mechanic at local motorcycle shops, Homer went to work for the Sacramento Municipal Utility District. There he served as a foreman. A quiet leader, he won the respect of those around him.

He never missed a chance to fly. He often took his children up in the air. He performed aerobatics. He worked doing occasional aerial photography. A devoted pilot, he owned several planes. Two of his friends had experimental planes they wanted him to fly. Carl Mueller built a 1911 Curtis Pusher replica that Homer flew in an air show. George Perriera, owner of Osprey Aircraft, built a one-seater to land in water that Homer flew. Homer had two children with his wife, whom he met while stationed in Australia.

Sacramento's Triple Ace pilot died from heart failure at age of fifty-six, after attending a World War II squadron reunion. The words (summarized) attributed to President Truman upon presenting Homer with the Distinguished Service Cross still make Sacramento proud:

> *The President of the United States takes pleasure in presenting the Distinguished Service Cross to Cyril F. Homer (0-732248), Captain (Air Corps) U.S. Army Air Forces, for extraordinary heroism in connection with military operations against an armed enemy while serving as Pilot of a P-38 Fighter Airplane in the 80th Fighter Squadron, 8th Fighter Group, FIFTH Air Force, in aerial combat against enemy forces on 3 April 1944, in the Southwest Pacific Area. On this date, Captain Homer shot down FOUR enemy aircraft in a single engagement. Captain Homer's unquestionable valor in aerial combat is in keeping with the highest traditions of the military service and reflects great credit upon himself, the 5th Air Force, and the United States Army Air Forces.*

First Triumph Man in Town: Joe Sarkees

Born 1915 in Wisconsin, Joe Sarkees was a son of parents originally from Syria. His father worked in a furniture factory. He had four siblings, all of whom passed away at early ages, although his two brothers lived until their forties. He attended Sacramento High School. In spite of these personal losses, there wasn't a scramble held in the Sacramento area that didn't find Sarkees in the middle of the action. Not only did he like to tease, but he also brought leadership to the motorcycle community. A founding member of the Fort Sutter Motorcycle Club, he organized gatherings and field games all over Northern California. He competed many times at the Sacramento Motorcycle Speedways from the relatively early age of eighteen.

A talented mechanic, Sarkees built Cy Homer a 1938/39 BMW to race at the 1940 Oakland two-hundred-miler. At the time of World War II registration, Sarkees worked for Al Lauer's motorcycle dealership. After serving in the army, he worked at McClellan Field. In the mid-1940s, he opened a motorcycle shop on the site of a former gas station at 16th and C. Sarkees sponsored riders and exerted leadership by sponsoring annual scrambles, drawing hundreds of riders. In later years, he told a newspaper reporter that he got his first dealership in 1945.

An old gas station at 16th and C became site of Sarkees's first business, where he sold and built models such as the one here, ridden by Homer at the Oakland Speedway. *Gaylene Tompkins.*

A Capital City Tradition

Whitie Tompkins sketched and painted the BMW built by Sarkees for Homer to ride in the Oakland two-hundred-mile. *Gaylene Tompkins.*

In 1948, Sarkees opened the Motorcycle Service Shop at 2525 Broadway. He became known as one of the first, if not the very first, Triumph dealers on the West Coast. European bikes filled a need that American-made bikes did not. Later he acquired Ariel, Ducati and BMW. He took on Mustang. He stocked cycles ranging in price from $269 to $1,700. "There was a time when we sold 25 cycles a year," he would tell a newspaper in the following decade. "Now we sell more than 200 each year."

Sarkees renamed his business Joe Sarkees Motorcycles as he became more prominent. He was a relentless advocate, insisting that motorcycles were the safest vehicle on the road. "Riders are more alert, more aware. They are in the fresh air," he once told reporter Al Calais of the *Sacramento Bee*. He described the pride in get-togethers for trips down the Sacramento River to Rio Vista or into the Mother Lode. "It's quite a sight, really—30 or 40 of us in our old units going down the river road, and at a pretty good clip, too…healthy and fun."

Each of Sarkees's bikes bore his exceptional handicraft. He possessed an uncanny expert ability mixed with a creative touch. "You get a part here and a part there. It sometimes takes five years or more to put one bike together. Sometimes you have to make a part that just can't be found and we all hate to do that because it really takes away from having the real thing."

Sarkees mentored many riders, including Shorty and Whitie Tompkins, Paul Albrecht and Rich Hardmeyer. The latter raced for him throughout

Albrecht was known for a winning smile and tough racing style. *Steve Tompkins.*

A Capital City Tradition

Left: National Champion Paul Albrecht represented Sacramento well in the "Greatest Sport in the World." *American Motorcyclist/Rich Hardmeyer.*

Below: Albrecht's Harley WR leaned into the curve within a wheel's length of Shorty Tompkins's Ariel at the Galt track. *Steve Tompkins.*

fell on the ground or he broke the bike. Albrecht was known be as tough as they came, physically and mentally, never failing to climb back into the saddle as long as his bike and body remained intact. A broken nose, crushed cheekbones, fractured ribs or a cracked limb were but mere annoyances to Albrecht. In 1941, when his bike split beneath him while racing at ninety miles per hour, he purportedly said, "Most of fellows in the business are pretty rugged. They have to be." Said one observer, "He's as hard a driver as there is. He guns his motor into a curve. He doesn't know what fear is."

Standing five-foot-five or five-foot-six, depending on the source, Albrecht believed that a rider with short legs had the advantage by taking command of the turns where it counted, angling forward and "out of the way." In his opinion, a rider could control the mount and pick up yardage over taller guys, who drag their legs for balance and traction. "There's a thrill in it I just can't describe," said Albrecht, who liked racing on stock factory engines on half-mile and one-mile tracks. He also raced on frames built for one-quarter-mile tracks. On June 25, 1950, Albrecht placed second at Bay Meadows in the twenty-five-mile National Championship. Later that year, he ran second in the Pacific Coast Championship at Vallejo in a twelve-lap three-fourth-mile race. Albrecht won many high-profile races, including the fifteen-lap race at Belmont. He won or placed in many national races from five to twenty-five miles.

In 1987, Sacramento recognized Albrecht by inducting him into the NorCal Athletic Hall of Fame. Three years later, the *Sacramento Bee* named him one of the city's one hundred top athletes. He lived all eighty-six years on his family's turkey farm at 65th and Broadway. When he died in 2004, a special grave marker appeared at St. Mary's Catholic Cemetery and Mausoleum: "MOTORCYCLE NATIONAL DIRT TRACK CHAMPION."

DUO OF ARTISTRY AND SKILL: WHITIE AND SHORTY TOMPKINS

Shining in Sacramento records are brothers Whitie and Shorty Tompkins, born Ross and Francis, respectively, in 1920 and 1921. They were as close as siblings could be. Although they competed in many races together, whichever of the two won didn't matter, for a win of one made the other happy. They spent their lives building, repairing and flying around racetracks and cross-country events. They once found themselves in the hospital at the same time following injuries from different races.

A Capital City Tradition

Above: Whitie and Shorty Tompkins rejoiced after winning first and second, respectively, at a Colfax meet. *Gaylene Tompkins.*

Right: Whitie Tompkins gave a preview of what he could do on an Indian Scout with special hill climbing modifications. *Gaylene Tompkins.*

The brothers attributed their success to Joe Sarkees. "He taught Shorty and me how to ride," said Whitie, "and he always watched over us."

Whitie participated in many Sacramento rides beginning in the early 1930s. From an early age, he also showed an affinity for sketching. His favorite subject: motorcycles. His eye for detail showed up in the racing photos, programs and paraphernalia he collected and organized. In keeping with his personality, he held on to a typed "Start List," which he reviewed before every race:

> *1 quart oil #50*
> *1 quart oil #30*
> *1 sets of spark plugs*
> *2 gallons of gas*
> *Sprockets*
> *Extra chains*
> *4 snap links*
> *Both tool boxes*
> *Carburetor*
> *Oil can*
> *License plate*
> *Registration slip holder*
> *Adhesive tape*
> *Rear stand*
> *Cotter keys*
> *Grease motorcycle*

Brother Shorty showed himself to be a true master at track competition; it was said that he won sixty-one out of ninety races and placed second or third in the rest of races he entered in one season alone. Everyone wanted to see Shorty race. In 1947, he won the world's quarter-mile dirt track record, with his brother, Whitie, right behind. He took the fifteen-lap main event at Bayshore Stadium and was, in fact, recognized for there for having amazed the most points in 1950.

In spite of his wins, Shorty refused to take risks. He remembered the days of the "suicide clutch" and no clutch. Once he told a newspaper that he waited for an opening instead of trying to enter a solid mass. Good equipment and skill were required for safety. Riders needed to recognize the type of tread essential for various surfaces. The bike had to fit the driver. "The most dangerous part of racing is being thrown or run over,"

A Capital City Tradition

Shorty (*left*) tore down the track on his Ariel to catch the Indian Scout in the middle. Belmont, 1948. *Jerry Bland.*

Shorty Tompkins flattened out to gain advantage on his Ariel at Bonneville. 1940s. *Steve Tompkins.*

Dirt flew as friends of Shorty Tompkins came down the track, with the Indian Scout leading at a Northern California fairgrounds. Wherever there was vroom and zoom, Shorty was not far away. *Steve Tompkins.*

Shorty once told a newspaper. "I was tossed onto the track. A cycle sped past me, took my pants and some skin with it. For a while I thought I was hurt seriously. Later I realized it was chiefly embarrassment." Shorty recalled that one crash left him feeling like a battering ram was smashing him into a wall. One widely circulated photo shows Shorty on his back flat on the track with his legs airborne. By 1950, he was known for his "winning ways" on the Capitol Speedway with a fifteen-lap event in the weekly racing program.

The brothers jockeyed back and forth in cross-country exercises at Glen Alder. Once, Shorty started behind his brother. Ten laps, each of five miles, with creeks, turns at unexpected times, ups and downs; Shorty won, with Whitie right behind. This outcome was typical, as the brothers dominated the pages of local newspapers' sports section.

Both siblings suffered long-term physical effects from the sport they loved. In Lodi, Whitie lost his left leg above the knee when he stopped in swirling dust to avoid hitting a rider. Another racer, not seeing through the dust, plowed into him. Shorty ended up with a limp. But like many Sacramento riders who loved their sport, they would not stop racing.

The brothers, talented mechanics in their later years, restored and collected bikes. Whitie died in 1988, Shorty in 2001.

Clipboards and Stopwatches: Carl Mankel and Ray Weser

Behind any race stood the dedicated crews that ran the operations: mechanics, pit men, announcers, track preparers, scorers and others. A nervous energy filled the minutes before every race: one last adjustment, filling tanks, checking the tracks and all the tasks that made the races go smoothly. These dedicated support teams watched over the riders accelerating, breaking and banking into turns, rolling and pitching, fighting the competition to get home first.

On almost any day of the week, two longtime motorcyclists officiated at races: Ray Weser, American Motorcycle Association state referee and, Carl Mankel, timer. Between the two devotees, they steered or presided over motorcycles for a century. They oversaw dirt track, tourist trophy, short track, lap races and wheel-to-wheel and incline battles of the great names. As riders donned their helmets, masks, goggles and numbers, Weser picked up his clipboard and Mankel a pencil, stopwatch and clock.

Weser, born in Sutter County in 1914, fell in love with bikes at an early age. He was quoted as recalling the first time he laid eyes on a hog, "dripping oil, spokes coming out of everywhere." Weser worked as a mechanic in Sacramento. Later, he became a district manager for Harley. In 2016, he was memorialized in an article, "101 Year-Old Veteran Takes Last Harley Ride with 50 Bikers Behind Him." Members of the Veterans of Foreign Wars and Grand Canyon Harley organized "One Last Ride" through the Prescott Valley in Arizona. Weser sat on the back of a new Tri Glide, driven around as a rare diamond accompanied by fifty cyclists roaring behind.

Mankel, of German parents, was born in 1899. A native Sacramentan, he attended Sacramento High School. In 1914, he joined the Capital City Motorcycle Club. In a Harley sidecar, he with Archie Rife broke a record traveling from Sacramento to Stockton. Originally a mechanic and for a short awhile in the motorcycle retail business, Mankel became a building contractor. He joined the Fort Sutter Motorcycle Club. Residing at 1316 I Street, he was lauded in a motorcycle publications for "perfect

Left: Ray Weser (*striped shirt*), an official American Motorcycle Association referee, loved motorcycles so much that he was gifted a last ride, at age 101. *Jerry Bland.*

Below: The Capital City Motorcycle Club assembled outside its clubhouse at 2414 13th Street, financed by Julius Kaminsky in 1948. *Magri Family Collection.*

A Capital City Tradition

Field meets at Glen Alder offered games, "eats" and trophies sponsored by the Fort Sutter Motorcycle Club. *Fort Sutter Motorcycle Club.*

electric timing." In 1949, Mankel attended a reunion of the Capital City Motorcycle Club, born from the Wheelmen and the Sacramento Motorcycle Club. Fourteen longtime members gathered, including Frank Murray (member since 1911); Fred Pearl, the boxing promoter (1896); Holy Cameron, the first Indian dealer (1910); Rife, who mentored Joe Petrali (1915); C.M. Goethe, an early Wheelman (1893); Chester Scott, who on a Jefferson aced races and hill climbs (1910); and William A. Langley, early Excelsior dealer (1920). Mankel died in 1952 at the age of age fifty-three and was buried at East Lawn.

Both Mankel and Weser belonged to the Capital City Motorcycle Club, which now had its own clubhouse, a twenty-five-by-fifty-two-foot rustic structure at 2414 13th Street, thanks to Irene and Julius Kaminsky, who also helped the Cyclettes finance their own clubhouse. Capital City members paid off a $2,000 loan with endurance and road runs, motorcycle polo and drill team appearances. A race on the Dixon fairgrounds in 1946 brought in $500.

BY THE LATE 1940s, both Capitol City and Fort Sutter Motorcycle Clubs were leading activities that appealed to a broad swath of enthusiasts. World War II veterans returned, anxious to hop on a motorcycle. Class C flat track racing exploded. European bikes were becoming the rage. New fencing, crash walls, bleachers and lights made a new track called Lazy J Speedway. After several years of sharing the midget car racing schedule at the Capital Speedway, hardtop racing flourished. But for the many motorcycle fans, there was no joy greater than the clash and combat of the two-wheeled burners.

SYMBOLS OF THE MID-CENTURY SACRAMENTO MOTORCYCLE SCENE

On hot summer nights, the Music Circus captivated Sacramentans under a tent with *Paint Your Wagon*, *Brigadoon* and *Oklahoma!* The Village Theatre and the Eaglet Theatre added to the arts sensibilities in a city filled with military defense and government employees. Tower Records and Country Club Center offered music and suburban shopping.

Frank Murray retired from the Harley business, making way for Armando and Lu Magri to take over the franchise, renamed Armando Magri Harley-Davidson Motorcycles. But Murray still entertained enthusiasts at his cabin in the foothills about ninety minutes from Sacramento. As a testament to the continuing evolution of motorcycle riding, Harry Smith Motorcycle Insurance Shop plugged services next to Joe Sarkees Motorcycles. Jack's Motorcycle Shop at 3401 Sacramento Boulevard advertised the Powell Scooter, foretelling the invasion of the light family scooter. Al Lauer traded his Indian franchise for BSA, Sunbeam and Cushman, but like musical chairs, these franchises would change from dealer to dealer German and Italian models gained popularity, although none compared to Triumph, BSA and Norton, the dominant brands until the invasion of the Japanese bike. By the late 1950s, Lauer, now with his son at the helm at 1830 J, was advertising DOT, NSU, Velocette and Francis-Barnett.

A group of riders interested in more competitive events formed a group called the Polka Dots. Charter members included Gordon Septinelli, Red Cadwell, Walt Vaughan and Jim Stowe. They loved bikes, and in addition to the many competitions they would hold, they relished the freedom of accelerating in rice paddies and chasing rabbits. The Fair Oaks Municipal Beach, a skill-based course, was "open to women." Northern California saw more interest in female ridership, although few organized races or clubs existed that were dedicated to women. The Sacramento Cyclettes remained a cherished club, even if more social than before. Irene Kaminsky remained involved, showing off that Sacramento female leadership with handouts and presentations, such as the following (from Lu Magri's scrapbook):

> *Members...we are known among the best clubs and definitely secure and independent in all respects....Go into this year with your hearts full of loyalty to our club—Just as our hearts are full of belief in each and every one of you. President, we trust you to handle our club affairs and to see that harmony and success prevails over every thought that should enter our club.*

Many other Sacramentans or events led motorcycling through the 1950s, including the following.

Hang-Out Place: The Calculator and the Sailor

Orrin Hall moved to Sacramento from Red Bluff in 1937. He started a butane distribution business for which he built a shop on his property, eventually inhabited by motorcycles. His first partner was Joe Sarkees, with whom he sold and serviced Triumph and Ariel bikes. Soon Joe took the new Triumph line, and Hall, working at Mather, took on new partner John Burdette. Employed at McClellan Air Force Base, Burdette lived in the Parker Homes military complex, a few miles away from Hall's home and shop filled with cycles.

Located at 1133 Bell Avenue, the business Hall-Burdette operated on a part-time basis, weeknights 6:00 p.m. to 10:00 p.m. and Saturdays from 10:00 a.m. to 6:00 p.m. On Saturday afternoons, in an adjacent vacant lot, cars would stop along Bell Avenue to view the impromptu races staged by the shop. The eight-mile dirt oval beckoned both experienced and new racers alike.

The business advertised repairs and service, all makes and models. Burdette participated in many races on a bike or behind the scenes. Soon the business took on Norton, Velocette and, in time, Royal Enfield, Matchless/AJS and Francis-Barnett. Some of the young men who liked to

A Capital City Tradition

Orrin Hall (*left*) and John Burdette (*right*) opened Hall-Burdette on Bell Avenue and later, Del Paso Boulevard. *Carol Sutherland.*

visit were Korean War veterans and saw themselves as "adapting to home after a rough time." Hall-Burdette was the perfect place to gather. Said one enthusiast, "There was also a group of would-be racers, known as 'the Norton Gang,' who hung out at the shop." As dealerships opened, Hall-Burdette focused mainly on Norton. It began tuning for Jocko Bennett, the

Hall worked on bikes of many riders, including Shorty Tompkins (no. 49), here with Sam Arena (no. 79) at Bay Meadows in 1950. *Carol Sutherland.*

Tompkins brothers, Red Cadwell and others. Sundays meant traveling to Reno and Bay Area races.

In 1957, Hall left his day job to make Hall-Burdette a full-time shop, newly located at 2211 Del Paso Boulevard. Burdette still worked part time at McClellan. They took on Parilla Motorcycles. Orrin became fascinated with the 250cc Parilla. A master at modifying motors and frames, he began to study the Parilla's inner workings. Using a slide ruler, he calculated ways to step up performance. He drilled holes through the frame, now named "the Gadget," to lighten its headway. New forks of titanium added to enhancements. In 1960, Orrin asked Norris Rancourt, a prominent local competitor, to ride the Gadget. With that request, Rancourt, the Gadget and Hall made history (see the section "Ride to the Future: Rancourt, Honda and the Gadget").

Hall's partner John Burdette, born in Nebraska, joined the navy in 1935. From the USS *Pennsylvania* in the Pacific, he was transferred to Pearl Harbor. There, enlisted men formed a band for which Burdette played the trombone. After leaving the navy, he returned to the family farm in Nebraska. One day, he saw a sign advertising jobs for aircraft instrument mechanics at McClellan Field. He and his wife spent their honeymoon on a Harley riding to Sacramento. When World War II began, Burdette enlisted in the U.S. Army Air Corps to train as a B-29 pilot at Thunderbird Field in Arizona.

Burdett's mechanical knowledge and hand-eye coordination helped him through. He was sent to bombardier training base in Deming, New Mexico. He also learned to fly B-17s and B-29s. Burdette never saw war and soon returned to McClellan. After meeting Hall, he worked at the shop at night while maintaining his day job.

In 1970, Burdette bought Hall out and ran the business until 1989. An accomplished sailor, Burdette participated in competitive events and belonged to the Lake Washington Sailing Club along with Cy Homer. Burdette also joined the American Arrow Flying Club at the Natomas Air Park. After forty years, he returned to flying.

BSA AND A LION: MOTORCYCLE SPORT CENTER

Everyone wanted British bikes, and no one wanted them more than Harold Ball and Elmer Graves, both of whom excelled at racing. As members of the newly created Polka Dots Motorcycle Club, formed in 1954, they opened the Motorcycle Sport Center, all makes and models, in 1955 at 2231 16th Street. Previously they worked for Al Lauer and, for a short while, Jim Reed Motorcycles. Ball and Graves's new Motorcycle Sports Center sold Ariel, Triumph Mustang, Matchless, AJS and, soon, BSA, a franchise they took over from Lauer. Both Ball and Graves participated in many runs and competitions, as noted in this excerpt from "Remembering Harold Ball, Elmer Graves, and Others" by Tom Green in the *Fort Sutter Motorcycle Newsletter* of October 2014:

> *Harold attended San Juan High School and began flat track racing, which was flourishing. He met Elmer competing in short track at Galt, Dixon, Stockton, Belmont, and Hughes Stadium. Elmer, almost six years older, had a sponsor, Casa Nello's, Mexican bar and restaurant just blocks from Hughes Stadium. Elmer suggested that Harold talk to Lauer, who had just become the local BSA dealer. So, in 1951 Harold went to work for Al and started riding BSAs. In 1952, Harold decided to go to Dodge City with the experts in the 50 mi, main event. Harold won. In 1953 Harold was off to Daytona to ride a BSA in the 100 mile Amateur race held on the old beach course "Team Harold" was low budget and knew there was no way he'd be able to carry enough gas to go the whole 100 miles. "He bought a small plastic bottle, filled it with gas and taped it to the frame." With only a few laps to go, Harold was leading but a lap or two later here he comes down*

Proficient racer Harold Ball showed off his 1950 650 CC Triumph before opening the Motorcycle Sport Center at 2231 16th Street. *Jerry Bland.*

the straightaway, the engine spitting and sputtering, fighting to keep control of the bike while trying to get the top off that bottle and pour gas into the tank. That slowed him down just a little too much and he finished in second place. Unlike today, most of the shops were selling motorcycles to young men interested in competition—field meets to enduros, scrambles to short track.

A Capital City Tradition

Harold and Elmer decided to open a shop—an old gas station at 16th and W. The Motorcycle Sport Center. They been open a few months before there were new BSAs on the floor and an Authorized BSA Dealer sign on the wall. Harold managed to keep racing. Besides Belmont and other local tracks he rode many national events. At Bay Meadows, he finished 5th in 1954 and 6th in 1955. Running a business was taking up a lot of his time—learned of birth of son on the starting line at the Santa Rosa Mile. They had to find something to replace the impending loss of BSA. They decided to become Yamaha dealers....By the early 70s the industry was awash in two strokes. By the mid-70s Harold sold his half of the business to Elmer. Harold bought a neighborhood-style bar, the Delta Club on J.

The Motorcycle Service Center, now run by Graves, advertised regularly until 1970. Along the way, Ball acquired a young lion he kept as a pet. The animal, named Chinook, would accompany him to a bar he owned. But after five years, Chinook came to the attention of local authorities. A Sacramento court ordered Ball and his wife to get rid of the 270-pound feline after he escaped his "compound" at Ball's Fair Oaks home. Ball maintained that Chinook was not much more than a big kitten—upon escaping his cage, he did nothing but curl up on a neighbor's porch to sleep. But officials didn't see it that way, knowing that the lion would grow to be 500 pounds. So Ball was forced to find his "kitten" another home. Thankfully, Lion Country Safari in Orange County promised a special place for Chinook, taking into account his special "domesticated" upbringing. Ball was said to be sad. Upon losing Chinook, he purportedly said, "It is better to have loved an animal—the lion—than to have never loved at all.

AMERICAN DREAM:
THE LITTLE SHOP BY THE TRACKS

In 1952, Jim Reed Motorcycles opened at 1520 16th Street, just yards from the railroad tracks on R Street. The small shop shuddered when trains passed. The business took over Indian motorcycles as production was nearing its end, but the brand remained "hot." Soon he added AJS, Matchless, Vincent and Francis-Barnett. When Reed took on the Lambretta, he advertised, "It's here, Italy's great Lambretta, smartest thing on wheels, extra 'car' for the entire family!"

Riders met outside Jim Reed Motorcycles at 1720 16th Street for a run to a Colfax field meet. *Jim Reed Archives.*

A native of Montana, Reed bought his first motorcycle for three dollars at age twelve from a farmer who couldn't get it running. The adolescent worked on it for hours and then hopped on when the motor sparked to life. At the bottom of a hill, the motor died. Upon following brother George to Sacramento in the late 1930s, Reed fell in love with Sacramento's warm climate and fresh fruits. In World War II, he served in the Battle of Okinawa, earning a Bronze Star and a Purple Heart. After starting his motorcycle business, Reed sponsored rider Roy Murray and participated in a few competitions himself. At a Selby Stables race, he fell on his head and lost consciousness. He was known at home for occasional daring acts, like the time he drove to L.A. all night in driving rain and freezing wind, with his brother-in-law hanging on behind, to attend a car show in Los Angeles.

At Jim Reed Motorcycles, the business model consisted of heavy print advertising. He sponsored "Indian Day" and exhibited at the Autorama and the state fair.

Reed celebrated each customer by taking a photo of every proud buyer on his or her motorcycle. For customers with children, he gave out "My daddy rides Indian" T-shirts.

A Capital City Tradition

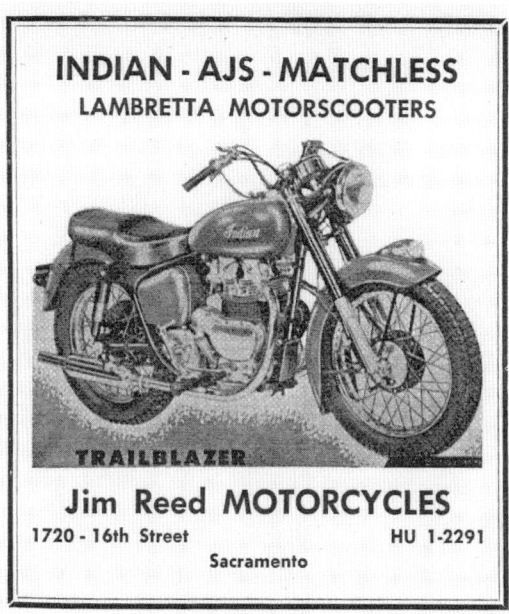

Above: At the 1953 state fair, Jim Reed displayed his models and banners, including Indian, Vincent and the Italian Lambretta, showing the diversification of some dealers of that era. *Jim Reed Archives.*

Left: While dealers differed in their approach to advertising, Jim Reed Motorcycles relied heavily on newspaper display ads. *Jim Reed Archives.*

Sacramento Motorcycling

Former employee Anthony F.J. Martinis recalled a farmer from out of town who came into the shop:

> *He asked for the biggest and most expensive bike on the floor. We couldn't tell how much he knew about motorcycles. After he bought a Bonneville Chief, he said he didn't know how to ride. Jim said to me, "Go out on the street on the side of the shop and teach him about the bike." I showed him how to start it, where the brake was, where the clutch was, the shifting lever, and then I rode it down the block to demonstrate. After that he got on the bike, started it, killed it a few times, then got it running down the street, and just kept going. We never saw him again.*

In the mid-'50s, Reed began to collect European cars he took in on trade. In 1956, he closed Jim Reed Motorcycles to go into the car business. He opened Cambridge Motors near Town and Country Village and sold Triumph under an iconic neon sign with a lightning bolt next to a Triumph TR3. Soon he secured the Alfa Romeo and Fiat franchises at Continental Motors at 16th and H and other locations. "Hobos" who traveled the trains would come by asking for him by name. Because they smelled like liquor, Reed would not give them money but would buy them dinner at the nearby Mansion Inn. He always remembered the man who returned many months later to repay him with a few coins.

Reed believed in business by handshake. He was known for driving sports car convertibles. While he never missed a weekly golf game, he knew how hard his generation had worked, and he knew the value of money. When teaching his son to golf, he maintained that the old clubs were as good as new expensive ones, even after his son won the Sacramento youth golf championship. Reed's last years in the car business found his showroom on the corner of Arden and Howe. A few motorcycles always sat in his home garage. At age fifty, he learned to pilot an airplane. He won many landing contests, flew cross-country numerous time and served as president of the Sacramento Valley Pilot's Association for a decade. Reed learned to juggle, tap dance, ride a unicycle and excel at pool. In his seventies, he often took off on a trail bike to explore old railroad tracks and "to go off and think."

A Capital City Tradition

MOTORLAND IN NORTHERN CALIFORNIA: THE AUTORAMA

Sacramento put itself again on the map when, in 1950, the Capitol Auto Club began an annual car show at Capital Chevrolet. How the Autorama started is best summarized by the Capitol City Auto Club "Thunderbolts":

> *We were a group of Sacramento area "Hot Rodders" with the common interest in racing their Model T. In 1950, while serving as president of the Capitol City Auto Club Thunderbolts,* [Harold Bagdasarian] *talked the members into having a show to settle friendly arguments over the outstanding merits of their personal customized cars. The Capitol Chevrolet dealership at 13th and K Streets was the site of the first gathering, which attracted 22 entries and 500 spectators. They took in $262 in two days at 74 cents a head.*

The enduring cheerleader of the Autorama was Harold "Baggy" Bagdasarian, born in Fresno. His father was from Turkey, and Bagdasarian became president of the Capital City Auto Club Thunderbolts. Every year, as the Autorama grew, he added new displays, including motorcycles, speed boats, accessories and speed equipment. By 1954, the event lasted three

Fort Sutter Motorcycle Club sponsored a display of bikes, raised platforms and mannequins portraying hill climbs and dirt track racing at the 1953 Autorama at the Memorial Auditorim. *Rich Hardmeyer.*

days and hosted more than one hundred entries, including from the CHP and the U.S. Air Force. The following year saw 150 exhibits after moving to the Food/Hobbies Building at the state fair. One section was converted to a theater seating 400 to show color films. By 1957, the Autorama attracted more than 2,500 visitors. The following year, more than $1,400 in trophies was awarded. By 1956, the show had increased to twenty-four classes of vehicles and five days in the Merchandise Mart building. A believer in showmanship, Bagdasarian knew how to mix "kid" entertainment and TV personalities. He would go on to include midget and short track cycle races in Cal Expo, eventually expanding to nine Northern California shows, including the Grand National Roadster Show, the World of Wheels in San Mateo, the Sacramento International Bike and Van Show and Street Machines at Cal Expo. Bagdasarian was a good friend of Jack Gormley, member of the Fort Sutter Motorcycle Club.

Tradition and Bravado: A New Attitude in Town

Sacramento had always been a town of traditions, but with veterans readjusting to life back home from the war, a composite new attitude was fermenting. *Life* magazine's dramatic coverage of the 1947 Hollister motorcycle melee melded with the 1953 Marlon Brando movie *The Wild One*. Then word circulated of a new Hell's Angels motorcycle club—in fact, members of the newly formed San Francisco chapter in jackets carrying the Death Head insignia visited Jim Reed's booth at the 1954 state fair. Local enthusiasts gathered at shops, downing coffee while surrounded by lines of bikes tagged for repair or taken in on trade. "We kind of thought we were something," said Martinis, who worked at Jim Reed Motorcycles. "Guys who rode, raced, repaired and talked motorcycles—with attitude."

Riding attire meant brown boots, jeans rolled up at the ankle, white T-shirt, black leather jacket and a cigarette dangling from the mouth or twirling between fingers. Sunglasses were definitely an asset. A bandana around the neck could be raised at a moment's notice to ward off dust, should a ride come along. Gloves added to the outfit for competitive events. Absent a helmet, caps did the job, thin billed or captain-like, sometimes with silver studs coordinated with studded saddlebags and fringed seat covers. Women wore slacks, but with magazines and ads still largely male-based, women were not considered a big motorcycle consumer base.

A Capital City Tradition

Attire aside, one's own bike was the best way to express individuality. Enthusiasts modified their bikes for maximum effect—a way to show life on the edge. They took great pride in their bikes.

Well-known mechanic and restoration expert Edwin "Spider" Hawtrey learned to ride from his father, a charter member of the Sacramento Motorcycle Club in 1911. Hawtrey Sr. placed third in a five-mile race at the state fair track attended by Seymour, Balke and other names of the era. Son "Spider" graduated from Sacramento High School. He served as a flight engineer during World War II after losing a brother in the 184th infantry of the National Guard. Spider worked as a mechanic at local dealerships and garages. He won a hill climb at Sloughhouse on an Indian Scout and served as president of the Fort Sutter Motorcycle Club. After fixing up his prized motorcycle, he bought a red Alfa Romeo sports car. He liked flashy, fast vehicles. As a member of the Sacramento Sports Car Club, he competed in rallies, hill climbs and autocross. During the 1950s, his interest turned to hydroplane racing. His "C" racing hydro *Orphan Annie* became a fixture at ceremonies between San Diego and

Leather jacket, cigarette and vintage Indian Scout modifications conveyed the style of the era, represented by Edwin "Spider" Hawtrey, son of a charter (1911) Sacramento Motorcycle Club member. *Jerry Bland.*

Pasco, Washington. The man who came from racing pedigree built model ships and airplanes and restored foreign cars. After a life "on the edge," Hawtrey returned to his real love: restoring classic motorcycles.

WHERE HORSES RACED MOTORCYCLES: SELBY STABLES

The horse stables of Carl and Dottie Selby on Fair Oaks Boulevard near Watt Avenue opened their property to thousands of children, looking for fun. The property also hosted horse shows, professional rodeos, "bird dog" trials, hayrides and picnics. Famous cowboy couple Roy Rogers and Dale Evans attended many events at the arena that seated up to 3,500.

On Friday nights beginning in 1955, the beloved horse property turned into an open race arena for two-wheeled competition, thanks in part to motorcycle dealer Al Lauer, who was a good friend of Carl Selby's. Spectators parked their cars in a long row across the field. To the side, gravel piles and machinery from Teichert's company cut a profile of a city still with open areas in many places. A mixed scent of gas, smoke, hay and horse manure

During intermission at Selby Stables, Carl Selby on the quarter horse Comet raced against Walt Vaughan on his Norton. *Kim Brown.*

filled the air. The Capital City Motorcycle Club, Fort Sutter and the Polka Dots saw sack and stake, run and ride, potato race and short speed races by prolific riders: Septinelli, Hardmeyer, Jones, Stowe, Green, Cadwell, Woodson, Rancourt, the Corders, Lauer Jr., Kremer and Murray. They hit the dirt and plowed like crazy. Jimmie Jones liked the Selby dirt because it was soft, allowing for good traction. Twelve clubs of the Valley Council of Motorcycle Clubs turned out for meets. During intermission, Carl Selby brought out a stallion named Comet to race a motorcycle.

When nearby Sierra Oaks Vista residents complained about the noise, dust and glare of floodlights, county supervisors summoned Carly Selby. Standing before them, he claimed that only eight races were held the previous year but that he would go along with any suggestions. A week later, the board reviewed homeowners' request to abate summer racing. Selby threatened to go back to breeding hogs if his ability to hold races were taken away, as the local motorcycle clubs needed to have place to race. He was allowed to resume, which he did for the next few years.

Agajanian and the Sacramento Mile

No track plunged Sacramento into the broadening national lens of new-era spectator racing more than the Sacramento Mile at the California State Fair. Promoter J.C. Agajanian—or Aggie, as he was called—grew up wanting to be a car racer. But this dream didn't make his father happy, so Aggie instead became one of the youngest car owners at age eighteen and soon a promoter. In the 1930s, he served as resident of the Western Racing Association. In his trademark cowboy hat, he became the first race organizer to present 250 U.S. Auto Club events, from midget races to the Turkey Night Grand Prix at Ascot Park in Gardena to champ car races. Agajanian went on to great fame, including bringing Indianapolis cars to the California State Fair. The oval that once saw Balke, Perry, Burns and Creviston now hosted the equivalent in Indy drivers: A.J. Foyt, Parnelli Jones and Bobby Unser.

But the real significance of Agajanian to the Sacramento motorcycle community came from his efforts to negotiate with local authorities to allow sanctioned national motorcycle racing to return to the state fair track, a privilege denied since 1915. Agajanian's work paid off. In 1959, after securing permission from both local officials and the American Motorcycle Association, he brought a nationally sanctioned twenty-five-mile race to the California State Fair track. This accomplishment

Above: J.C. Agajanian, race promoter extraordinaire in his signature hat, flashed a smile with winner Carroll Resweber at the state fair at the AMA Grand National on July 19, 1959. *Chris and Cary Agajanian Collection.*

Opposite: Known as "Mr. Orangevale" for his many wins, Rich Hardmeyer easily graduated to the twenty-five-mile National Championship at the Sacramento Mile, where he competed on his 500 CC Triumph several years later. *Rich Hardmeyer.*

A Capital City Tradition

returned local racing to its roots. Soon would follow the fifty-mile AMA Grand National at the hometown oval.

Aggie lived in Beverly Hills. He died in 1984 and was inducted into the Motorsports Hall of Fame of America and the American Motorcycle Association Motorcycle Hall of Fame.

MORE THAN NIGHT SPEEDWAY: TRACKS AND HARE SCRAMBLES

If Selby Stables was considered first in a series of 1950s night speedway locales, Mather Speedway was the second. Located off Excelsior Road past the Jackson Highway, Mather saw many sets of wheels, primarily lightweights. Corder, Hardmeyer, Rancourt, Murray, Moore, Kremer, Taylor, Albrecht and Barton were but a few of the warriors who crouched over handlebars to clash with contenders before 1,200 spectators.

Third in the night speedway series was 3 Star Raceway, off Watt Avenue near McClellan Air Force Base. Vince Bertolucci, whose father owned

Sacramento Motorcycling

Bertolucci's Body and Fender—he built some of the best Triumph Cubs while becoming a legend in hot rod customization—remembered attending 3 Star every Friday night at a young age: "We lived right across the street. You could hear the roar of the motorcycles on the track and see the glaring lights. There was nothing more exciting to a kid."

The story of 3 Star Raceway was best told in writing on February 25, 2017, by Michael Blanchard, writer and publisher of RustMag.com, after interviewing local rider Jimmy Jones:

> [T]hree tracks laid out concentrically, with the two inner tracks paved and the outer track dirt. The paved rings were for midget cars, the dirt track for motorcycle racing.
>
> In 1958, guys like Dan Haaby, Rich Hardmeyer, Chuck Barton, Ray Huff and the Corder family, as well as Jim Jones, were the stars of Three Star. Some of these guys also raced bigger Grand National bikes on the big tracks.
>
> Local shops like Joe Sarkees' and Al Lauer's were active in the scene and some of the better riders worked at the bike shops. Rich Hardmeyer and Benny Clausen worked at Sarkees' and Lem Corder was head of the shop there.
>
> The races were run for motorcycles in 50cc, 125cc, 200cc and 250cc engine sizes only because the track was less than a half-mile in length. The most common bikes used in the larger classes were Triumphs until the onslaught of Japanese bikes mid-1960s. There were also a number of bikes from the continent as well. Bultaco, Parilla, Ducati and Aermacchi/Harley were all represented. Small Hondas, Yamahas and Italian bikes dominated the smaller classes.
>
> Dick Bertolucci sponsored a couple of Triumph cubs in the 200cc class. His father Mario built the engines and he had some of the best riders of the day. Chuck Barton, Butch and Gene Corder, and Al Lauer Jr. all rode for Dick at one time. Gene's rival at the time was Dan Haaby and his Bultaco. The Spanish screamer was the fastest bike on the track for a while and more than a match for the Triumphs. Dick remembers that Gene complained that their Triumph shook badly when on the power. Mario took the engine apart and discovered that the crankshaft wasn't balanced well enough so he got out the knife-edges and set to work.
>
> Jim remembers owning the first Bultaco in Sacramento. One of his racer friends brought a Sherpa up from the bay area and ran it at Three Star. Jim liked it so much he decided he had to have one of his own. He tried to get Joe Sarkees to order him one but Sarkees didn't think much of the Bultaco so he wouldn't order it. So Jim went to Al Lauer and got him to order a 200cc Sherpa. He still laughs as he remembers uncrating the bike and finding it with mud all over it. At the time, Bultaco test-rode its bikes before shipping them out.

A Capital City Tradition

Cartoon sketches of races regularly appeared in the *Sacramento Bee*, as this one did April 26, 1957.

The Sherpa proved to be a very fast bike and Jim raced it for a couple of years. One night, during a race Dan Haaby crashed in front of him. Jim went over Haaby's downed bike. He went over Rich Hardmeyer, who Haaby had taken out when he went down, and flying into the air, went over the top of the six-foot wall surrounding the track. He landed on the other side with his

Right: John Puthuff led a fellow competitor coming off a jump at the Orangevale Scrambles. *Jimmy Jones.*

Below: Polka Dots founding member George Woodhouse on a Matchless 500 CC led Jim Reed and another rider at a Fort Sutter scramble. *Jim Reed Archives.*

Bultaco, a broken wrist and a split helmet. The bike was sold on after the wreck and Jim moved on to enduro racing and gave up racing at Three Star.

While night speedway kept Sacramento roaring, almost every day during the week found riders at Orangevale, air strips and fairgrounds up and down the Sacramento and San Joaquin Valleys. Some riders called Rich Hardmeyer "Mr. Orangevale" because, as one fellow racer recalled, "he won there every time." "Red" Cadwell, another star racer, loved Orangevale and hit it with a vengeance. He told his son, "If you aren't crashing, you aren't going fast enough." With Lazy J destined to close, the Capital Speedway offered tempting tracks. The Polka Dots, the new club in town, sought "100% competition," vowing to participate in thirty field meets, scrambles and enduros. Any farm, creek bed or hilly terrain belonging to Shultz, Diaz, Winkleman, Sartain and Roberts became arenas for mud runs and Hare Scrambles. All the usual riders and then some showed up: Eggers, Mann, Clawson, Graves and George Woodhouse along with others aforementioned.

Fun Ride in Sacramento: Hap Alzina's Playboy Scooter

Throughout the decades, the influence of motorcycles showed up in the hands of children, whether cast-iron toys, *Popeye* cartoons or books with a motorcycle theme. In the mid-1950s, an exciting new toy came to Sacramento when West Coast Indian distributor Hap Alzina imported the gas-powered, white-wheeled Playboy Scooter from Germany. "The Backyard Playboy Motor Scooter," weighing forty-two pounds, carried a one-cylinder, two-stroke Praenafa engine. Jim Reed, of Jim Reed Motorcycles, bought one for his children. The engine screamed and discharged dark smoke and steered like a real cycle on grass and cement alike.

Alzina's good name held special meaning in Sacramento. He had raced here many times in the early 1900s. In 1922, he bought out the Oakland Indian dealership of E.S. Rose; a few years later, he became the Northern California Indian distributor—soon the entire state. By 1948, Indian sales in Alzina's territory accounted for more than 20 percent of Indian's total worldwide. The man who loved Indian did everything possible to keep the factory afloat. Eventually, Alzina bought the western states distribution rights for BSA motorcycles. Under Alzina's direction, BSA's western distribution went from 3 to 265 dealers in twenty states.

Ross Alzina, grandson of legendary Oakland Indian and later BSA distributor Hap Alzina stood with the Playboy Scooter in an ad that appeared in automotive and motorcycle magazines. *Ross Alzina Collection.*

Known for integrity and hard work, Alzina was inducted into the Motorcycle Hall of Fame in 1998. Once, when asked if he viewed motorcycling as more business or pleasure, Alzina purportedly said, "Motorcycles are a business…I call it 40 years of fun."

THE COLDEST RIDE: RACE TO OLYMPIC VILLAGE

After paying $40,000 for the TV rights for the 1960 Squaw Valley Olympics television rights, KCRA arranged to drive film to Reno and then fly it by light aircraft to Sacramento for processing and broadcast. Three days before the opening ceremony, blizzard conditions threatened the plan. When CBS found itself in a pinch, it knew the man to call: Armando Magri, of Sacramento's Harley business. In Magri's own words:

> *One day before the opening, KCRA news director Dave Hume called me. He had been worrying about driving the film through a blizzard to Reno, and asked if I thought a motorcycle could deliver it to the airport any faster. I had many miles of experience riding in snow, and told Hume I would be willing to try, "but why not bring it directly to Sacramento," I asked. "That would be considerably faster." He took me up on the offer.*
>
> *I rode a used Harley 74" with a windshield, saddle bags, and a lap apron. I brought a skid chain for the rear wheel. It was February 20, 1960. I had to stop and install the skid chain 60 miles up, at Gold Run. It*

A Capital City Tradition

snowed almost all the way. By the time that chain was on, my hands nearly froze. A Highway Patrolman said, "You're riding too fast. You had better tone it down from 55 mph to 35 mph. That's the legal limit with chains." I explained everything; the TV station, the news director, the film, the lens, opening ceremonies. He let me go on, saying only to be careful.

The ride down old Donner Summit got intense because road conditions became slippery. Half way down I passed a Cadillac with three girls in the back. They waved to me and I waved back. When I looked ahead, there was a snow plow in front of me. I hit the brakes too much and, wham, the bike slid right out from under me. The Cadillac stopped and everyone came out to help, but I felt foolish.

Approaching Squaw Valley, a string of cars was backed up for three miles outside of Truckee. The road was an icy mess, with deep ruts, which tipped me over. Picking up the bike, pushing it, starting it up, doing all the usual tasks, became even more difficult. Nevertheless, the motorcycle enabled me to ride between cars, and make my way to the front gate of Squaw Valley. There were NO PARKING signs all over. But a guard found a place to park. I told him "keep an eye on it for me, will you?" "Yes sir, yes sir," he said, as if I was some kind of a big wheel.

Magri, with film packed in his Harley FL "panhead" saddlebag, prepared to leave Olympic Village with cargo that would send TV coverage worldwide. *Magri Family Collection.*

There were about 47,000 people at the Winter Olympics that day. After filming the ceremonies, Harry handed me four rolls of 16mm film and took a couple of photos with me and the Harley. He said "Good luck, Armando," and I headed for Sacramento.

It was 3:30 pm. It snowed like crazy for the first part of my return trip. But like that race in Marion, Indiana, I decided this was one of those times to let it all hang out. The snow turned into rain at Blue Canyon, where I pulled over to remove the skid chain. Then, it was full bore straight to KCRA. Once at the station, I ran up to the newsroom and handed the film to Dave Hume. The time was 5:41 I had made the trip back in 2 hours and 11 minutes. It was easily the coldest ride I ever took. The film was developed and edited in time for airing on KCRA's early evening newscast. That was the first TV showing, anywhere in the world. KCRA scooped the CBS network by an hour and a half. When CBS executives asked how KCRA got the film so fast, we said, "by motorcycle."

Ride to the Future:
Rancourt, Honda and the Gadget

When Orrin Hall of Hall-Burdette built the bike he called the Gadget and needed a rider, he called on Norris Rancourt, known for the racing repute he had built riding similar bikes. The Gadget was a 250cc Parilla, Grand-Sport, considered by some to be the most successful Parilla racer in North America due to Hall's unique modifications. Rancourt became the rider to beat on the West Coast. In 1962, he scored the most points in the American Federation of Motorcycles road racing. He led the Gadget—or the Gadget led him—to more than eight Grand Prix and road racing titles in one year. Norris, Orrin and the Parilla proved to be insurmountable when they trounced all but one of the factory Harleys and Yamahas at the American Motorcycle Association's Daytona race.

Back home, Rancourt became Sacramento's first Honda dealer and the twenty-ninth in the United States, located on Fair Oaks Boulevard at the corner of California Avenue. Rancourt took on a few other motorcycle brands, such as BMW, Norton, Yamaha and Montesa. For several years, he raced cars and then went into the car business. Carmichael Honda Motorsports, Segway of Sacramento and Roseville Honda Autosports were but some of Norris's businesses.

Rancourt and the Parilla stood at the gateway of a new epoch: the invasion of the Japanese and other imported models, highly organized motocross

A Capital City Tradition

Norris Rancourt, Sacramento's first Honda dealer, prepared to fly on his 250cc Parilla Grand Sport A, known as "the Gadget," at the Cotati Raceway. *Norris Rancourt.*

spectaculars, carefully customized engines and frames and stylized wear guaranteed to appeal to a coming generation of gladiators.

LOOKING BACK ON FIFTY MAGNIFICENT YEARS

More than two dozen riders who raced in Sacramento occupy a name plate on the wall of the American Motorcycle Association's Hall of Fame. Each decade brought its own legion of riders, dealers, industry leaders, pit crews and fans who added their own marks. From the Wheelmen to the Sacramento Motorcycle Club and the Capital City Motorcycle Club, to Fort Sutter and the Polka Dots, these clubs and their direction and structure brought fun, camaraderie and competition that influenced areas well outside Sacramento.

Our own story makes us proud. After more than a century, our history echoes the memory of Reed Orr, who paid the ultimate price, and E.M. Brown, the cop on the one-cylinder model. Gone but worth appreciating are the Wheelmen gavel, Kimball-Upson catalogues and the Kodak cameras that Langley used to capture excursions. Emil Fabian, who brought three models to an afternoon competition and scored well on all three, lives on in newspapers archives. While we'll never again see Hardy Tompkins, whose Mexican grandmother lived to 107, we know the Jefferson that made him a celebrity. We can read about Archie Rife, a champ hill climber, and Al Lauer, who roared through flaming walls when not racing, showing horses or wheeling-dealing at meets. Joe Petrali left his likeness in the history books. Frank Murray's foresight

SACRAMENTO MOTORCYCLING

Jimmy Jones (*right*) on his DOT with a Vierra engine (with Roy Murray). He was known for his "retro" checkered helmet with the colors green and gold. *Jerry Bland.*

thrust us into the national speedway spotlight. The Sacramento Cyclettes took women's participation into their own hands. Magri, Homer, Albrecht, Sarkees and the Tompkins brothers cleared the path for newfound race techniques for skill, speed and spraying mud to make the audience gasp. The dealers of the 1950s—Hall, Burdette, Graves, Ball, Reed, Lauer, Magri and others—offered places to talk, dream and find friends, if not a racing sponsor. To Rich Hardmeyer, Jimmie Jones, Norris Rancourt and many others, we tip our hats.

Today, the sport of motorcycling embraces everyone, young and old, of every background. Women race, repair motorcycles, ride them all over the world and write books about them. Children watch televised races and run on real tracks. Clubs devote themselves to specialized competitions. A sport that in some decades attracted a large but particular segment of the community is now richer due to the diverse experiences of enthusiasts. Many form and participate in riding groups tailored to their unique interests. How far we have come since the racers ate pie between laps at Agricultural Park and the pedal fell off the first police motorcycle.

While the early bikes call out for our attention, the real story is best told by the men and women whose set jaws and steady grips gave motorcycles their true meaning. In any subsequent history, new people will be profiled and new bikes described, but no stories told will be as memorable as those from the first fifty years.

SELECTED BIBLIOGRAPHY

AMA Racing Archives, Pickerington, Ohio.
American Motorcyclist Archives. Various issues/dates.
The Antique Motorcycle Magazine. Various issues/dates.
The Art of the Motorcycle. Solomon R. Guggenheim Museum exhibit, June 26–September 20, 1998.
Automotive Industries Ltd. *Bowman: The Horseless Age*. Trade magazine, 1917.
Avella, Steven M. *The Good Life: Sacramento's Consumer Culture*. Charleston, SC: Arcadia Publishing, 2008.
———. *Sacramento: Indomitable City*. Charleston, SC: Arcadia Publishing, 2003.
Baker, Erwin G. "How I Made the Three-Flag-Record: Inside Story of the Dash from Canadian Border to Mexico." *Motorcycle Illustrated* (September 1915).
The Bicycling World and Motorcycle Review. Early issues.
Bruno, Lloyd. *Old River Town: A Personal History of Sacramento*. Sacramento, CA: Suttertown Publishing, 2002.
Burg, William. *Sacramento Then and Now*. Charleston, SC: Arcadia Publishing, 2007.
California Highway Patrol Museum. Various displays on CHP history.
Capital City Motorcycle Club Archives. Capital City Wheelmen.
Center for Sacramento History. Capital City Wheelmen scrapbook and records and Sacramento Cyclettes scrapbooks and ledgers.
Collier's (assorted years, including 1915). Numerous issues.

Selected Bibliography

Cycle World (July 1917).

DeWilde, Amanda G., and James C. Scott. *World War I and the Sacramento Valley*. Published in association with the Special Collections of the Sacramento Public Library. Charleston, SC: The History Press, 2016.

Ensanian, Armand. *Discovering the Motorcycle: The History, the Culture, the Machines*. N.p.: Equus Potentia Publishing, 2016.

Hepting Collection, Center for Sacramento History.

Holmes, Tony, comp. *"Twelve to One" V Fighter Command Aces of the Pacific*. Oxford, UK: Osprey Publishing Ltd., 2004.

The Horseless Age. April 24, 1912. Automobile trade magazine.

Krehbiel, Andrew. "101-Year-Old Veteran Takes Last Harley Ride with 50 Bikers Behind Him." The Delite, September 28, 2016. thedelite.com.

Linder, Will B. "The California Snow Carnival." *Overland Monthly* (January 1920).

Lord, Myrtle Shaw. *A Sacramento Saga: Fifty Years of Achievement—Chamber of Commerce Leadership*. Sacramento, CA: Sacramento Chamber of Commerce, 1946.

Magri, Armando. "Then and Now." Autobiography, limited distribution, 1995.

Matthews, Alice Madeley. *I Remember the House Where I Was Born: Memories of Days Gone By*. N.p.: Sacramento Country Day School, 1984.

Mattos, Rick. *California Highway Patrol*. Images of America Series. Charleston, SC: Arcadia Publishing, 2008.

Motter, Tom. *Sacramento: Dirt Capital of the West*. Rancho Cordova, CA: Vintage Images, 2009.

Ostrander, Rich. "John Burdette, July 24, 1916–March 6, 2007." *Fort Sutter Newsletter*, March–April 2007.

Pacific Motorcyclist. August 14, 1913, and other issues.

Rafferty, Todd. *The Complete Illustrated Encyclopedias of American Motorcycles*. Philadelphia, PA: Running Press, 1999.

Renstrom, Richard. *Motorcycle Milestones*. Vol. 1. Caldwell, ID: Classics Unlimited, 1980.

Richardson, Mike, and Sue Richardson. *Wheels: The Magical World of Automotive Toys*. San Francisco, CA: Chronicle Books, 1998.

Sacramento Bee. Issues from 1906 to 1960s.

Sacramento City-County Library System. Sacramento Room records.

Sacramento Police Department files. Sacramento, California.

Sacramento Union. Issues from 1906 to 1922.

Scheide, R.V. "Armando's Last Ride." *Sacramento News & Review*, May 24, 2001.

Schilling, Paul. "Killa Parilla." *Cycle World Magazine* (January 2006).

Statnekov, Daniel K. "Pioneers of American Motorcycle Racing." N.p., 1998.

Wagner, Herbert. *Harley-Davidson 1930–1941: Revolutionary Motorcycles and Those Who Rode Them.* Atglen, PA: Schiffer Publishing, 1996.

Willis, William Ladd. *History of Sacramento County.* N.p.: Historic Record Company, 1913.

Wilson, Hugo. *The Ultimate Motorcycle Book.* N.p.: DK Adult, 1993. Published in association with the Motorcycle Heritage Museum. 1993.

Winterhalder, Edwards, and Wil De Clerico. *Biker Chickz of North America.* N.p.: Blockhead City Press, 2010.

Wyman, George A. "Narrative Across America." *American Motorcyclist* 36, no. 4 (Winter 1997).

Partial List of Websites

http://blog.modernmechanix.com/playboy-motor-scooter
http://goodoldsandlotdays.com/gallery/kimball-upson-co
http://www.americanflattrack.com/news/view/2015-marks-the-50th-running-of-the-sacramentomile-ama-pro-grand-national
http://www.capitolautoclub.com/historicalinfo.html
http://www.motorcyclemuseum.org/halloffame/detail.aspx?RacerID=146
http://www.motorcyclepediamuseumorg
http://www.mshf.com/hall-of-fame/inductees/joe-Petrali.html
http://www.norcaldragracing.com/drag-strips
http://www.pictame.com/user/journal.artist/2906925517
http://www.rodshows.com/sa/show-history.html
http://www.statnekov.com/motorcycles/lives22.htm
http://wwwdairylandclassic.com/amatimeline.html
https://thevintagent.com/2018/03/01/class-c-racing-in-california-1935
https://www.cyclechaos.com/wiki/Armando_Magri
https://www.indian-motorcycles.com/hap-alzina-indians-man-of-the-west
https://www.motorcyclistonline.com/chasteen-tops-oakland-class-c-meet
https://www.rustmag.com/blog/2017/2/25/three-star-raceway-w6e4z

INDEX

Capital City Wheelmen 7, 22, 24, 26, 28, 39, 60, 61, 64, 66, 67, 156, 169, 181
Carter, R.H. 30, 53
Catlett, Bud 77
chariot races 110
Clayton, Frank 73
Cottrell, Jack 100, 125, 135
Creviston, Ray 52, 55, 59, 88, 171
cross-country relay 57

D

Del Paso Country Club 8, 32, 42, 73
De Rosier, Jake 19, 49

E

Elder, Wayne "Sprouts" 74, 88, 99, 100, 101
Elkus, Albert 8, 22, 37, 50, 56

F

Fabian, Emil 27, 50, 51, 52, 55, 57, 59
Fair Oaks Municipal Beach 158
Farwell, Freddy 55
Faulders, George 86, 88
Federation of American Motorcyclists 40, 53
Fical, C.A. 38
Fical, Howard 39, 63, 66
Fort Sutter Motorcycle Club 11, 106, 116, 142, 153, 168, 169
Freitas, Bernadette 122, 127, 130
Freitas, Clem 130
Freitas, Lamar 130

G

Gadget, the 160, 180
Galloway, Dick 24, 33, 38
Graves, Elmer 161, 177
Greer, Walt 68

H

Haggin Oaks Golf Course 132
Hale Brothers 22, 130
Hall, Orrin 158, 180
Hardmeyer, Rich 143, 171, 173, 177
Harrison's Cyclery 39
Hawtrey, Edwin "Spider" 169
Heft, Schubert Ferdinand 58
Hess, John 59, 61
Homer, Cy 100, 117, 138, 140, 142, 161

J

Jacobsen, Marjorie 126
Johns, Don 19, 51, 52, 55, 59, 88
Jones, Frank M. 39
Jones, Jimmy 174

K

Kaminsky, Fritz 69, 122
Kaminsky, Irene 8, 122, 132, 156
Kaminsky, Julius 8, 122, 132, 156
K. Breuner's 79
Kiessig, Harry R. 28, 40, 64
Kimball, Moses Nixon 31
Kimball-Upson 8, 17, 21, 31, 42, 47, 53, 55, 61, 69, 81, 84, 88

INDEX

L

Lamoreaux, Wilbur 100, 101, 102
Landreth, Mittie 8, 28
Langley, William A. 7, 17, 19, 21, 22, 33, 36, 38, 42, 43, 50, 66, 88, 92, 97, 156
Lauer, Al 67, 102, 106, 112, 113, 114, 116, 142, 161, 170
Laughlin, Bud 100, 112, 130
Lazy J Speedway 156
Leuders, Billy 59
Lindbergh, Charles 72

M

Magri, Armando 15, 100, 101, 104, 106, 110, 125, 135, 157, 178
Magri, Lu 132, 137, 157, 158
Mankel, Carl 61, 80, 125, 153, 156
Mather Speedway 173
McCarthy, Leo 49, 57, 80
Middlemiss, Thomas 52
Mossman, Putt 113, 114
Motoraid 40
Motorcycle Day 51
motorcycle polo 109, 156
Motorcycle Week 54
Motormaids 121
Municipal Motorcycle Officers of California 77
Murray, Frank 61, 67, 69, 81, 97, 98, 99, 114, 121, 124, 132, 134, 135, 137, 156, 157
Murray, Gladys 61, 86, 121, 122, 132, 133
Murray, Roy 164
Murray, Sybil 122, 125, 132, 133

N

Nichols, Phyllis 129
Nixon, Richard 74

O

Orr, Reed 22, 24, 26
Orr, Scott 8

P

Pearl, Fred 26, 60, 97, 156
Perkins, Dudley 49, 57, 58, 83, 84, 88, 89, 98, 109, 125, 145
Perry, Robert 19, 51, 52, 55, 59, 77, 171
Petrali, Joe 80, 88, 89, 90, 91, 92, 93, 97, 100, 116, 156
Pixley, Clarence 26, 51, 53, 66
Polka Dots 157, 171
Post, C.N. 24, 26
Putzman, Emil O. 8, 36, 42, 57, 66, 67, 97
Putzman & Hoffman 8, 35, 36, 43, 57

R

Rancourt, Norris 160, 171, 173
Reed, Jim 161, 163, 177
Rhyne, Gene 102
Richards, James 64
Rife, Archie 61, 67, 80, 88, 89, 90, 92, 93, 97, 153
Robinson, Dot 121
Ruhstaller, Frank 22, 51

INDEX

S

Sacramento Auto Show 99
Sacramento Mile 171
Sacramento Motorcycle Club 7, 21, 22, 24, 26, 40, 60, 64, 94, 169, 181
Sacramento Motorcycle Speedways 99, 142
Sarkees, Joe 100, 106, 141, 142, 143, 145, 150, 157, 158
Schnitzer, Ewald 112, 114, 117
Scott, Chester 21, 22, 24, 27, 40, 156
Selby, Carl 116, 170
Selby Stables 116, 164, 170, 173
Septinelli, Gordon 157, 171, 177
Seymour, Ray 19, 169
Speer, Finnegan 86
Speer, Pat 84
Stahlman, Mildred 116
Stillo, Mario 117, 135
Sydenstricker, E.E. 124

T

ten Bosch, Adrian 26
Tharp, Harry 64
3 Star Raceway 174
Tiechert, Adolph 64
Tompkins, Francis "Shorty" 104, 114, 117, 143, 148, 150, 152, 153
Tompkins, Hardy 7, 22, 37, 41, 50
Tompkins, Ross "Whitie" 114, 143, 148, 150, 152, 153
Trapper, Dick 49, 50

U

Upson, Stu 8, 17, 21, 31, 32, 33, 42, 81, 97

V

Vance, Myla 126, 129
Van Guelder, Hector 125
Vaughan, Walt 157

W

Weinstock, Harris 22, 28
Weinstock Lubin Cup 52
Weser, Ray 153, 156
Western Federation of Motorcyclists 26, 49
Woodhouse 177
Woodson, Frank A. 7, 80
Woodson, Joseph A. 24

ABOUT THE AUTHOR

Native Sacramentan Kimberly Reed Edwards was introduced to motorcycles before she could walk. Her father owned a small motorcycle shop near the railroad tracks in downtown Sacramento. She grew up understanding the rider's passion and love for the sound and scent of a bike firing up. She compiled this history to honor the Sacramentans who shaped the early motorcycle craze, beginning with the Capital City Wheelmen, early dealers, downtown merchants and a group of ardent riders who formed the Sacramento Motorcycle Club in 1911 and later clubs. As president of the California Writers Club and a former "Writing Personal Histories" seminar leader, Kim has inspired people to write their own accounts, believing in the value of communities telling their stories. She has written articles and essays on topics such as lifestyle, travel and seniors. She holds an MA in education and is an alumna of the Kenyon Review Writers Workshop and the Squaw Valley Community of Writers. Kim retired from the California Department of Education, where she coordinated programs for teachers and schools. She has three children, three grandchildren and cats Nacho and Tofu.

Visit us at
www.historypress.com